# HOME IS THE HERO

# HOME IS THE HERO

*A Play*

BY

WALTER MACKEN

LONDON
MACMILLAN & CO. LTD
1953

PRINTED IN GREAT BRITAIN

THIS PLAY TO
THE ABBEY THEATRE
THAT OLD LADY
WHO DESPITE FRIENDS AND ENEMIES
REFUSES TO DIE

This play was first produced by the Abbey Theatre at the Queen's Theatre, Dublin, July 28, 1952, with the following cast:

| | |
|---|---|
| Paddo O'Reilly | Brian O'Higgins |
| Daylia, *his wife* | Eileen Crowe |
| Willie, *his son* | Mícheál O hAonghusa |
| Josie, *his daughter* | Ite Ni Mhathúna |
| Dovetail, *the tenant* | Harry Brogan |
| Bid, *his wife* | Máire Ni Chatháin |
| Mrs. Green | Bríd Ni Loinsigh |
| Lily Green, *her daughter* | Siobhán Ni Eaghra |
| Trapper O'Flynn | Eamon Guaillí |
| Manchester Monaghan | Liam O Foghlú |

Produced by Ria Mooney

# THE PEOPLE

PADDO O'REILLY          DOVETAIL, *the tenant*
DAYLIA, *his wife*          BID, *his wife*
WILLIE, *his son*          MRS. GREEN
JOSIE, *his daughter*          LILY GREEN, *her daughter*
TRAPPER O'FLYNN          MANCHESTER MONAGHAN

---

# THE PLACE

The general downstairs living-room in a house in a long
avenue of houses in the town of Galway

---

# THE TIME

The present

*You hear a tapping noise. You wonder what it can be. Then you know when you see the young man in the room bent over the last. He is nailing a sole to a shoe. He is mainly seen with your left eye. Behind him an open door leads into the street. The late afternoon sun is shining on the red-brick floor. Along from the door there are stairs leading upstairs until they are lost to sight. There must be a window up there because there is a light shining down the stairs. The stairs are covered with a narrow strip of linoleum, highly polished and wearing away. If you do not go upstairs you can continue down the narrow passage to the latched door at the end. It leads into the yard outside and if you were caught short in the night you would use this door, because Councils who build houses for the poorer classes think a toilet in the yard is better than none at all and damn good enough for you. You have to go out there too to get water from the tap. It would have cost a few shillings extra to have brought the few yards of pipe into the kitchen. The ratepayers could not afford that. The passage is formed by the staircase on the left and the wall of a room on the right. It is a bedroom. You can hardly see the door. It is around the bend of the passage. The rest of the wall of the kitchen at the back is the width of this room. There is a wall cupboard hung on it, with glass doors. It holds a few pieces of good china, two Toby jugs, one cracked, eggcups, canisters for tea and sugar, butter on a plate, jug of milk. Under the cupboard a long wooden bench. You can sit on* this, or step on it if you are too small to get the things out of the top shelf of the cupboard. The fireplace is in the middle of the other wall opposite the front door. It is a spacious fireplace, with a tall grate and two hobs, highly black-leaded. The surrounds of the fireplace are picked out in painted red brick with white lines all around the joins. There is a thick mantelpiece over. It is so cluttered up that you find it hard to discover what is on it. There are two china dogs anyhow, supercilious-looking beasts, not mongrel types. There is also a lamp, a red one, lighted to the picture of the Sacred Heart above the mantelpiece. For the rest, packets of Woodbines, matches, small baskets holding threads and needles. Letters and a few books. There is a stool on either side of the fire, rough-wooden, highly polished from human seats. There is a wooden table in the centre of the floor, seeming to suffer from pernicious anaemia it is scrubbed so white. There are four wooden chairs near or about it. They are scrubbed very clean too. There is a picture of a buxom woman and a pleased-looking man with a moustache and a high collar hanging on the wall below the front door. She is in black and wears a cameo brooch. He has a high collar and a tie-pin. The whole place looks clean and well cared for. There is green distemper on the walls and a paper border all around just under the ceiling.

The only thing to disturb the order is the litter around the young man working at the last. He is sitting on a chair. He wears a leather apron. The last is resting on a stout, narrow, wooden box. There are two drawers nailed to each side of it, one holding tools, the other nails. The young man is black-haired. It is falling over his eyes as he hammers. He reaches a thin hand occasionally to push it back. He *has the small nails in his mouth and transfers them from there to the leather as he hammers them home. He is in his shirt-sleeves. His arms are thin-looking, but lithe muscles are active in them from his hammering. His face is pale and narrow and when you see his eyes you will notice that their deep-setness accentuates the narrow face. He does not look up when the latch is raised on the back door and a middle-aged woman with a shawl rushes into the kitchen. She has a parcel in her hand. She is an old edition of the woman with the cameo brooch, inclined to stoutness. She throws off the black shawl and drapes it over the banisters. She is wearing a grey cardigan tucked into a black skirt with a check apron over. She is breathing hard. Her face is red.*

THE WOMAN. All but didn't get it, I did. The mane hound! 'Me husband comin' home after five years,' I says, 'and you begrudge me a bit a black pudden.' (*She decants the parcel on the table, disclosing the round of black pudding, and six sausages.*) 'Mrs. O'Reilly,' he says, 'I'd give you enough black pudden with a heart and a half to sink a battleship if you'd show some signs of payin' for all the black pudden already consumed by you, owing to me, and I have to live too, don't I, and when will the brave Paddo be home?' He softened up after a while. People are very good when you give them time. (*Looking up at the clock as she grasps the frying-pan which is hanging on the wall beside the fire.*) Sweet heart, look at the time. He'll be on top of us before we are ready for him. Where's Dovetail? Has Dovetail gone with the car? Where's Josie? Why didn't she come home for her tea? My God, is nobody about to help a soul at a time like this? What will Paddo think of us? (*She slaps the pudding on*

3

*the pan.*) Willie, do you hear me talkin' to you?

WILLIE. I do, Mother. (*He spits the nails on to his hand.*) I can only answer one question at a time, and only then when I have no nails in me mouth. As far as I know, Dovetail is still upstairs and Josie is up in her room and I don't know why she didn't come for her tea; and now excuse me, if I don't get Finnegan's shoes done we don't eat to-morrow. (*He puts the nails back in his mouth. Just then a shrill voice calls from the landing above.*)

VOICE. Daylia! Daylia! Are you athin, agirl? Willie! Willie! Is your mother athin?

DAYLIA (*going over to the bottom of the stairs*). Yes, yes, I am, Bid. What is it? The time I had gettin' the bit a mate for Paddo out of your man; if it was a young wan with a bit of leg he'd give it fast enough. Is Dovetail still up there? Why isn't he gone with the van? Doesn't he know that the train'll soon be above?

BID (*coming down the stairs, a small little woman with a wizened face, thin arms with the cardigan sleeves rolled on them, a canvas apron around her*). Amn't I tryin' to get him into his dickey and the language is awful! It's no use, Daylia, Dovetail'll never move on big occasions without his dickey. He says to meet Paddo without his dickey'd be like facin' his Creator without a habit. I'm just tellin' you.

VOICE (*from above*). Bridget! Bridget! Where the hell are y'? What are you doin' with the gab-gab-gab and I near stranglin' meself? Will you come up, woman? Isn't me stud after flyin' into the charlie?

BID (*giggling*). Wouldn't he kill yeh? That's the way he's been since the day I married him. Never got out a napkins, he hasn't.

4

DAYLIA (*shouting up*). Dovetail! Dovetail! Hurry up, will yeh? Do yeh want to be late, do yeh? What'll he say if there isn't a soul to meet him?

DOVETAIL. All right, all right, all right. Amn't I hurryin'? Isn't there bags a time, isn't there? Bridget, will you come up, will yeh?

BID. Comin', comin'! That man!

DAYLIA. Is Josie up there?

BID. She's in her room above. Beautifyin' herself, I bet, for the return of her father.

DAYLIA. Josie! Josie! Come down, I want yeh. (*She goes back to the fire.*)

DOVETAIL. Bridget! Bridget! Will you come up, will you?

BID (*going back up*). What a happy day!

DAYLIA. You know what's worryin' me now, Willie?

WILLIE (*through the nails*). What?

DAYLIA. Your father. He never knew we had Dovetail and his wife in as lodgers since he left. Nobody told him. What could we do? We had to live, didn't we? They give 's ten bob for the big room, don't they? How else could we have lived, tell me?

WILLIE. Dunno.

DAYLIA. Well, there, we did. But he's a proud man. I don't know if he'll take to it. But what could I do? Five years ago. Ye weren't earnin' a copper then. What could I do?

WILLIE. Nothin'.

DAYLIA. God help 's, it's a hard life.

JOSIE (*who has come down the stairs fixing a beret on her brown hair. She is wearing a red coat with a blouse and skirt under it. She is well built, with rather thick lips, a handsome*

5

*more than good-looking face. She goes over behind her mother, looking into a mirror to fix the beret.*)  Well, Mother, what's wrong with you?

DAYLIA (*jumping*). Jesus Mary 'n Joseph, you startled the senses outa me.  Why don't you make a noise when you come up on a person?

JOSIE.  There's enough noise going on in this dump without me making more.

DAYLIA.  Why weren't you in for tea?

JOSIE.  Because I had it out.

DAYLIA.  Don't speak to your mother like that.  Where are you goin' now?  Are you going to the station to meet your father?

JOSIE.  No bloody fear.

DAYLIA.  Josie!

WILLIE (*spitting out the nails*).  That's no way to talk.

JOSIE.  You shut up!

DAYLIA.  Be careful, me girl!  You're big enough now but you're not too big to have the handle of a brush across your backside.  Wait'll I tell your father about your goin' on while he was away.

JOSIE.  Tell away.  It doesn't worry me.  A lot he cared about us or he wouldn't have ended up the way he did.  'And where's your father, little girl?'  'He's doin' five years' hard labour down in Limerick, sir, but please give me the job all the same.  I'm not like me father.'

WILLIE.  Your father had nothing to do with you being in and out of about ten jobs in a few years.  You change your jobs like you change your admirers.

JOSIE.  You shut up.

DAYLIA (*pleading*).  For the love of God let us have peace for this day.  Let us forgive and forget.  It wasn't

6

your father's fault, Josie. Everyone knew that. It wasn't like Paddo. Didn't even the poor oul' judge say it wasn't his fault? Can't we let it rest? It was a terrible pinance for an active man like Paddo to be closed in like that like an animal.

JOSIE. It wasn't half the price of him, and if he thinks he'll come back now and find his daughter waiting for him with her eyes misty with tears, then he has another think coming. I'm going out and I'll be back in me own good time, and if there's any fuss I'll be out and staying out for good. And you can tell that to me father when you see him (*she is at the door now*), and if he doesn't like it he can lump it! (*She is gone.*)

DAYLIA. What in the name a God's got into her?

WILLIE. She has her side, Mother. Kids are cruel. They make you suffer. Many a time in a row Josie has been called a murderer's gosling. She'll get her own back, on the wrong person; probably him.

DAYLIA. I don't understand half of what you're saying, Willie. How could them street arabs go around calling her a murderer's gosling? You know well Paddo was no murderer. Everybody knew that. Why should they be sayin' things like that? It was an accident like everybody said. If he was a murderer would they have only given him five years? You shouldn't be tellin' me things like that. Think of all the things I had to put up with.

WILLIE. I was only trying to explain Josie, that's all. She'll change. She feels that it's his fault that she had such a bad time growing up. After all she's only nineteen. That's the proud age. You don't expect a nineteen-year-old to be lit up like a Christmas tree because her father is coming home from jail.

7

DAYLIA. Oh God, I'm distracted, so I am. The time I had rearin' that one, and no Paddo around to give her the strap. Think of me, can't ye? Think of the time I had in five years to get a bit to put in yeer mouth. The things I had to do. He won't know all that. He'll expect everything to be just the same. (*She goes to the stairs again.*) Sweet God, he'll be above and not a sinner to meet him. Dovetail! Dovetail! Are you comin' or goin', man. Listen to the tick of the clock, can't yeh?

DOVETAIL (*upstairs*). Comin', comin'! You can rely on Dovetail, Mrs. O'Reilly. (*He comes down the stairs trying vainly to shove the front of the dickey inside his waistcoat. He seems to float down the stairs. He is a smallish man with a ripe fifty-year-old face, decorated by a clipped moustache that makes him look a bit like Genghis Khan. The suit he is wearing fits him only where it touches him. The bottoms of the trousers are bunched around his shoes. He wears no tie with the dickey, and on his head he is wearing what was at one time a shooting-hat.*) I never missed a train in me life even if I had to catch it be the skin a me teeth. Man, we'll put up a great show, so we will. All the oul' butties will be at the station and the kids have been learnin' a song to sing in the street. When the first darkness falls we're goin' to light a bonefire under the lamp. He'll never forget his comin' home.

WILLIE. Maybe he'd be better without the celebration.

DOVETAIL. What, man! Are you transfixed? Is it let the man sneak in the back like a rat in a drain? Doesn't everyone love him? Isn't he a proper hayro? This'll be a bigger do than the May procession.

DAYLIA. The time is tickin' away, man.

8

DOVETAIL. Hurry. Isn't the oul' tin can outside the door rarin' to go? I'll g'out now and kick her in the carburetto. (*He goes out, still trying to fix his dickey.*)

DAYLIA. That man'll be the death of me.

BID (*coming down the stairs pulling a black shawl about her*). I thought we'd pay up the rent a biteen early this week, Daylia, knowing that times is short. Here you are. Dovetail ran over a young pig outside Ballinasloe and when there was no one around to claim the corpse he flogged it to a butcher in Athenry.

DAYLIA. It's very obliging of you, Bid. Are you sure ye can spare it?

BID. We can't, agirl, but you know how Dovetail is. If he has ten bob in his pocket he says it drains him of ambition.

DAYLIA. Since it is so prompt maybe we'd go down the road and get a few bottles of stout for Paddo. It'd be a terrible thing to have him comin' into a dry house. What do you think, Willie?

WILLIE (*looking at her peculiarly*). Do whatever you wish, Mother.

DAYLIA (*on the defensive*). They's no need to look at me like that. Anyone would think it was out to get drink for meself I was.

WILLIE. I didn't say that, Mother.

DAYLIA. You looked it. (*Noises outside the door are heard of* DOVETAIL *trying to crank up his van.*) I had to have something to keep me strength up all the time your father was away, but to see you lookin' at me you'd think I'd turned into a drunkard.

BID. God bless us, what a thought! *You* don't drink. A bottle a Bass'd blind yeh. Dovetail was readin' a bit outa the paper to me about how an odd drop of stout is good for your marrow.

DOVETAIL (*coming in, a bit red in the face*). The bitch is lettin' me down after all that time and the very minnit I want her. Have you a drop a paraffin in the house, Daylia?

DAYLIA. There's a bottle here.

DOVETAIL. That oul' yoke hates petrol. Would you believe that? She has to have a drop of paraffin in her before she'll warm up. Thanks, agirl, I won't be a shake now. This'll fix her up. (*He goes.*)

DAYLIA. So we'll just slip down, Bid, and get a few bottles for him. I might just take one meself to put heart in me. Will you look after the pan, Willie?

WILLIE. I will.

DAYLIA. We'll be back long before he comes. I'm excited, you know, Bid. It's like the time when we were coortin'. (*She is putting on her shawl.*) I used to work in the big house in Taylor's Hill. I never thought the hour'd be up until he'd be outside the gate waitin' for me. Oh, a big fine strong man he was. We used to wander over be the bushes in the quarry. He'd take off his short coat and be doin' handsprings for me. He was a fine man.

BID. Paddo could always go, I'll say that for him. Full of fire he always was. Didn't they nearly throw him out of the union, he was workin' so hard?

DAYLIA. Heart-scaldin' it's been all those years without him. Nobody'll ever know what it has meant to me, to be without him so long, and not a penny piece comin' into the house except bloody charity. He'd kill me if he thought I took charity. But what could I do? All those years.

BID. Pride fleeth before a slack belly, Daylia.

DAYLIA. No man in Ireland was as proud as Paddo. Couldn't he lift a hundredweight in each hand?

BID. He was the pride of the Transport and General Workers. Weren't all the skivs in Galway cracked about him? Didn't I admire him meself? I cried for a fortnight the morning after ye were married. Dovetail for me was a sort of booby prize.

WILLIE. The wooden spoon.

DOVETAIL (*coming in*). Even now after the paraffin, the cursed goddam thing won't stir. I'll rattle her, wait'll you see. I'll give her something up her jersey. Give's a hammer, Willie, a goddam heavy hammer. I'll bust her bowels, honest to the sacred God I will. (WILLIE *hands him a hammer. He goes out muttering.*)

DAYLIA. It'll be the miracle a God if that fella ever gets to the station. Listen to that. (*Heavy banging is heard.*)

BID. He'll cripple that oul' van. It's a good van. Dovetail is very fond of that oul' van. He says he has it since it was a wheelbarra. I don't know how he keeps it goin'. He has a genius for engines. There, didn't I tell you? (*as the engine outside bursts into sporadic life*).

DAYLIA. We better be goin', Bid. We'll be just there and back in time before Dovetail has him down from the station.

DOVETAIL (*coming in triumphantly*). She's just like all the women, that one out there. If you don't kick them you get no good of them. I'm off now, Daylia, and look at the time. Plenty of time we have. What did I tell ye?

DAYLIA. Good man, Dovetail. God bless you. I don't know what we'd have done without you the years. Don't forget the pan, Willie. (*She goes out the back.*)

DOVETAIL. Where are ye off to, Bridget?

BID. We're just goin' down for a little message, Dovetail.

DOVETAIL. Well, blow the top off it first.

BID. God, Dovetail, you're a comic. (*She follows* DAYLIA.)

DOVETAIL. Them two. It's a wonder their faces don't turn black. You wouldn't like to come up and meet Paddo with me, Willie?

WILLIE. I can't, Dovetail. These are Finnegan's (*holding up a shoe*). There you see to-morrow's dinner.

DOVETAIL. Well, I don't know. It seems quare the man comin' in up above and not a sinner of his own to meet him. Of course I'll make him a speech of welcome, and the Panther and God Save the King and Munge Arab'll all be above, but it's not like your own. It's not every day we have a hero comin' back to the street. I wouldn't wonder the Mayor ought to be up there too. Look at the fame the man brought's? Wasn't his name in all the papers in the country?

WILLIE. Your sense of values is distorted, Dovetail.

DOVETAIL. If that means what I think it means you don't agree with me, is that it?

WILLIE. I don't think Paddo is a hero. He probably won't think so himself.

DOVETAIL. That's where we don't dovetail, Willie. We part there. Now listen. What happens? He strikes one blow in a fair fight and your man drops dead. You couldn't ha' done it betther with a humane killer.

WILLIE. He was a man, Dovetail, not a beast.

DOVETAIL. Didn't he die in a good cause?

WILLIE. You better go and catch the train.

DOVETAIL. No argument? Well, no man is a hero to

## Home is the Hero

his own as they say. I'll be off so. I'll round up the kids. We'll have to have the street lookin' like the first race night before we finish.

> *He goes.* WILLIE *pares a bit of leather off with his long sharp knife and then goes over to the pan. As he walks you notice that he has a bad limp, that his right leg is shorter than his left one. He has almost to contort his body. He stirs the stuff on the pan with a fork. Outside you hear* DOVETAIL'S *van chugging obscenely away, and then a girl comes in the door. She pauses a while looking at* WILLIE. *She has a pair of shoes in her hand. She is young, well-favoured, and is dressed in a jersey and skirt as if she had just stepped out of her own house to come here.*

THE GIRL. Hello, Willie.

WILLIE (*turning to her, a look of pleasure lighting up his face*). Why, Lily.

LILY (*coming in a bit*). What are you at?

WILLIE. Stirring up black pudden. It's for my father's tea.

LILY. Oh, you're makin' an awful mess of it. (*She leaves the shoes at his bench.*) Give me that fork. (*He relinquishes it.* LILY *stirs the fire under the pan.*) Have you no hot plate on the hob? You'd make a poor husband, Willie.

WILLIE. I'll get one. (*He takes a plate out of the cupboard, hands it to her.*)

LILY. It'll be strange for you having a father at his tea.

WILLIE (*going back to his bench*). Yes. Are these your shoes? (*Picking them up.*)

LILY. They are. Are they gone to hell or will you be able to make anything of them?

WILLIE. I'll fix them. You have a small foot.

LILY. Thanks. (WILLIE *laughs*.)

WILLIE. We can make a bit of profit on the people with small feet. Use half the leather, charge the same price as a big foot.

LILY. Yeer terrible swindlers. Your father will be home soon?

WILLIE. Yes.

LILY. Isn't it a wonder ye haven't the table laid out nice or something? Where's your mother?

WILLIE. She's gone down the road for a message with Dovetail's wife.

LILY. These messages! I'll lay it. Is there a clean cloth anywhere?

WILLIE. Last Friday's newspaper is on the stool.

LILY. She must have a real cloth somewhere.

WILLIE. Try the cupboard, the top shelf. (*She stands on the bench, reaches up.* WILLIE *admires her shapely legs*.) That's a nice leg you have, Miss Green.

LILY. Thank you, Mister O'Reilly. Do you add a few pence for compliments?

WILLIE. No. Compliments are thrown in to keep the customer happy.

LILY (*coming down with a white cloth. She shakes it out and puts it on the table*). It's grand to get something for free.

WILLIE. Were you dancing last night?

LILY. I was.

WILLIE. Did you have a good time?

LILY. The usual.

WILLIE. Wish I could dance.

LILY. I'll teach you.

WILLIE. I'd look sweet. Here's me head, me ah is comin'.

LILY. Know what I like about you, Willie?

WILLIE. I'm a damn good cobbler.

LILY. No. You're not sorry for yourself.

WILLIE. Where does that get you?

LILY. That's just it. Nowhere. Josie was at the dance.

WILLIE. Oh. Who was she with this time?

LILY. Manchester Monaghan.

WILLIE. She can pick them.

LILY. Manchester is no good to anyone.

WILLIE. Even his own mother would agree with you.

LILY. Josie is gone a bit wild, Willie. Why?

WILLIE. She has a complex. All the kids jeering after her. You know how cruel kids can be. They called me Hoppity as well. But I didn't mind. That can't cure you or make you any worse.

LILY (*taking down cups and delf from the cupboard*). Ye'll be having your tea with him. I'll put for the four of you.

WILLIE. Skip one. Josie is in revolt.

LILY. Oh. Willie, were you always lame?

WILLIE (*looking at her, startled*). No, I wasn't. I don't remember a time I wasn't, but I was born whole.

LILY. What happened?

WILLIE. It's only hearsay evidence. You remember Paddo?

LILY. I do. He was a nice man. We used always wait for him in the street on a Friday night when he got paid. He always dished out a bag of sweets. I thought he was a giant. Whenever we'd read about giants in school, the good giants that wouldn't hurt a sinner, I always thought of Paddo. He was always great life, wasn't he?

WILLIE. He was. Full of bounce, that was Paddo.

The only time he could sit still was when he would be playing draughts with the Trapper. Great laugh, great songs, great stories. He'd make you sit up. He was like holding a charge of electricity.

LILY. That's right. He always made your heart jump.

WILLIE. You ever see Paddo with babies? He loved babies.

LILY. He seemed to love everybody.

WILLIE. He had a way with babies. He used to hurl them into the air and catch them lightly in his arms as they came down. He did that to me when I was a baby, but he didn't catch me once on the way down. It was pay night. He had a few drinks taken. That's what happened my leg. It grew a bit short.

LILY. Oh. (*She looks at him. His head is bent over his work.*) Do you resent Paddo, Willie?

WILLIE (*looking up and thinking*). No, Lily, I don't. If it had happened when I was big and could remember, maybe I might. But you get used to a short leg when you've never remembered any different. Besides it did things for me. When you can't go out you stay in. I learned to read after we left school. That's what I spend my money on. Some day I will show you my books. (*He looks at her. There is a tense silence in the air.*) Do you resent Paddo, Lily?

LILY. Do I resent Paddo?

WILLIE. After all he did kill your father, didn't he?

LILY (*after a pause*). Yes, he did.

WILLIE (*after another pause*). And now you are laying the table for his tea.

LILY. Yes, that's right. It's a strange world, isn't it?

WILLIE. What made you come, Lily?

16

LILY. Paddo coming home brought it all back to my mother. She's crying away below in the house. I had to get out. I don't think it was really Paddo's fault. Even if, five years in jail for a man like him was a terrible punishment.

WILLIE. Your father was a nice man. He was a nice, quiet, inoffensive man. Why should that have happened to him?

LILY. I don't know. He was such a nice quiet man that he was hardly missed. Is that a strange thing to say?

WILLIE. I don't know.

LILY. Well, it's true. I was only thirteen then. His memory is gone now. All I remember of him is sitting in the corner reading a paper with a quiet smile at you. He hardly ever raised his voice. We got on. Brian has a good job and I have one. It's just the same as if he had never been with us, except that sometimes my mother cries in the night. She wakes you up at it.

WILLIE. I see.

LILY. I think it's past and the sooner we forget it the better. It might make Paddo feel better to see we're not dodging him.

WILLIE. I see.

LILY. But there's something else. How long have you known me, Willie?

WILLIE. All my life.

LILY. All your life. That's right. I hear you sometimes working at night. When I'm lying in bed with the street light shining in the window I can hear the tap of your hammer.

WILLIE. I'm sorry about that.

LILY. And when I'm passing by your house I know

17

that you are inside bent over the last. I can see the bit of hair falling over your forehead.

WILLIE. I haven't time to be combing it.

LILY. Willie, if we let things go on and on, do you think you'd ever get to the point of saying that you like me very much and that you wish to marry me? (WILLIE's *hammer drops to the floor. He stares at her.*) Well, would you?

WILLIE. For Christ's sake, don't talk like that!

LILY. Why wouldn't I talk like that? If I don't talk like that, do you think that you ever will?

WILLIE. Lily, what are you saying?

LILY. I know you are lame and that you've never been with girls and don't go to dances, and that you are not fit to have a wife, and that no girl would look the side of the road you are on on account of your affliction, and that your father killed my father in a drunken brawl in a pub, but nevertheless I can't help it. I can't get you out of my mind, and dances are no good when you are not there and all the rest of it, and there you are, I can't help it no more than you can, so we better get it over. (*She has her back to him.*)

WILLIE. I don't know what to say.

LILY (*crossly*). Well, say something, after I'm making an exhibition of myself.

WILLIE. I have always thought about you.

LILY. Pretty feeble.

WILLIE. What the hell can I say? Haven't you said everything? Haven't I run over it all in my head thousands of times, but I never even dreamed . . .

LILY. I knew it. You'd never have said it out. (*Turning to him*) Would you?

18

WILLIE. No, I would not. Who but a madman would even think it for two minutes?

LILY. Then it's all settled.

WILLIE. But Lily . . .

LILY. I know. How are we going to live, etcetera? I don't give a damn. Your father is home now and he can work and you don't have to be supporting them for the rest of your life. You can support me from now on, and how you go about it is your business. I've done all the spade-work and, Mister O'Reilly (*going over to him*), if you only had the smallest notion of how happy I am. (*She puts out her hand, brushes the hair back from his forehead with her fingers.*) I'll buy you a good comb.

WILLIE. God in heaven, Lily! This is fantastic. It's . . . look at me hands full of beeswax and grit and dirt so that I can't even lay one on you.

LILY. To-night. When your father is home you go and wash yourself and put on your new suit, and I'll put on mine and we'll go for a walk, Willie, and look at the moon, and God knows you should have enough to tell me then. Good-bye now. I'm off. I can't wait another second or I'd go all soft and somebody'd be in on top of us with a pair of lousy shoes and we'd be disgraced. I'll be back after tea. Mind yourself and think of me and find your tongue.

> *She is gone and* WILLIE *is left alone like a pilotless ship at sea. His face is a plethora of different emotions sweeping across it. He doesn't hear the old man coming in behind him, a bent old man wearing a long coat that is gone green-mouldy from use and a bowler hat which he removes to disclose white hair. He is carrying a box and a folded draughts-board under his arm.*

19

THE MAN (*with a disappointed look around*). So he's not back yet. (*He notices that* WILLIE *hasn't heard him. Speaks louder.*) I see your father's not back yet, Willie.

WILLIE (*half-noticing him*). Yes, that's right, Trapper.

TRAPPER. Well, is he or isn't he?

WILLIE. Is he or isn't he what?

TRAPPER. Home?

WILLIE. Who?

TRAPPER. Your father. Is there something up with you, Willie?

WILLIE. Oh, I'm sorry. Something up with me. No, not a thing, not a damn thing, just me whole life and three or four miracles. What's that you said now?

TRAPPER (*shaking his head*). You seem to be in a tiswas, Willie. Finnegan told me to tell you he will want his shoes in the morning. He has to go to a funeral.

WILLIE. To hell with Finnegan. I hope he busts a gut. I hope the corpse gets up and bites his corns. What funeral? Whose?

TRAPPER. Oh, a fur-coat funeral. The poor woman, the Lord have mercy on her. Finnegan used to scrape her drains. He was an odd man up there for a while until he got six months for whipping lead off the roof. So your father is not back yet?

WILLIE. Not yet.

TRAPPER (*going over to the stool below the fire*). I'm glad. I was afraid he would have come. I want to be sitting here like this with the draughts-board all set be the time he comes in. (*He draws the other stool down in front of him, places the draughts-board on it and lays out the men.*) Ye all missed Paddo, I know, but I bet none of ye will ever know how much I missed him.

WILLIE. Why not ? As long back as ever I can remember you and him played draughts on Mondays and Tuesdays. Why would I forget that ?

TRAPPER. That's right. Mondays and Tuesdays. That was two days out of the week. When you get old like me, Willie, you have all the days counted up. Nobody could play draughts with me like Paddo. Paddo had the batin' of me in every finger of his hand although you wouldn't think he'd be payin' any attention at all. I missed him sore. If I ever had a wife, I would have missed her less than Paddo. That's true.

WILLIE. Well, you can play away now.

TRAPPER. That's right. I'd ha' gone to jail for the two nights a week if they let me. Is that his tea on the pan ?

WILLIE. It is.

TRAPPER. It'll be fried to a frazzle. I'll put it on a plate and cover it.

*He gets a plate from the cupboard, empties the pan onto it, leaves the plate on the hob and covers it with another plate.*

WILLIE. You were never married, Trapper ?

TRAPPER. Never outside of a nightmare, Willie.

WILLIE. Did you ever think of what you missed ?

TRAPPER. No. I didn't have to think about it. All I had to do was to look around me at what I missed.

WILLIE. But that's part of the good part of it, Trapper. All the things that go wrong with some people. That's the fun of it to see that nothing goes wrong with you. Did you never see a girl in the middle of a cloud, Trapper, with the edges of the cloud all pink kind of and misty ?

TRAPPER. I can't say I ever did, Willie.

WILLIE. But that's what you missed, Trapper. Ne'er a one at all, all your life?

TRAPPER. Ne'er a one, Willie. When I was young I used to ride horses. Would you believe that to look at me? I wouldn't give a young horse with a delicate fetlock for all the women in Connacht. I'd rather a kiss from a young racehorse than to be nubbled be the Queen of Sheba.

WILLIE. All I can say is that I'm sorry for you, Trapper. You give me a pain in me heart I'm so sorry for you thinking of what you missed.

TRAPPER. Somebody got under you, Willie?

WILLIE. I don't know what's got under me. Did anything ever happen to you that was sensational, Trapper? Something so good that you could never believe it?

TRAPPER. Wait now. Ther' did. The year back that Pansy won the Galway Plate with me up on her back.

WILLIE. God, I don't mean oul' horses. Haven't you a single contact with a human being that med you walk in the sky?

TRAPPER. No. The nearest thing would be the night about twenty years ago that I bet Paddo in a game of draughts.

WILLIE. God scald you, Trapper, you must be the most bloodless man in the whole country. Like a fish you are.

TRAPPER. Was it Lily Green that set you moving, Willie?

WILLIE. Would you like me to talk about her?

TRAPPER. No. You have it all in your eyes. She's a nice girl. It's a pity about her father. Will that never come agin ye?

WILLIE. Why should it? Won't it make up for it to

22

her in a way ? I will fill a gap created by my own father.

TRAPPER. People will think it queer, I suppose, but then people are queer anyhow, so everything is even. Will your father feel happy looking at his daughter-in-law ?

WILLIE. My father will never have to look at his daughter-in-law. If ther's one thing living in this street has taught me, it's something that should be writ in neon signs over every sky in the land. Don't live with your mother when you're a father.

TRAPPER. It's a bad game. It's put up the brewery dividends no doubt and hotted up hell. So you will fly the nest ?

WILLIE. That's right. Isn't it a miracle ?

TRAPPER. Why so ?

WILLIE. God, look at her, Trapper, and look at me. I never even thought she'd look the side of the street I was on.

TRAPPER. You want to think betther of yourself, Willie, a game leg never bothers a cock. You're a good parcel over the leg. You have the stuffin', Willie, that's the thing. You always know people with the stuffin'. One look I could take at a horse. He might have a backside like a hawthorn tree but the stuffin' would be in him. I hope ye'll make a do of it, but keep away from Paddo.

WILLIE. I'll do that.

TRAPPER. All these people expect Paddo to be the same now when he comes back as when he went away. Do you expect that, Willie ?

WILLIE. He'll have to be a bit different, I suppose.

TRAPPER. You think over it for ten minutes and you'll see. I badly want to see Paddo. That's why things must be normal for him. That's why I have this board laid out like this, so that when he comes in he'll take a look and mebbe imagine it's just an ordinary Monday before he went away.

WILLIE (*tackling one of* FINNEGAN'S *shoes again*). That's a charity of you.

TRAPPER. Is it? I don't know. Most charity things spring from our own selfishness. That's a quare thought. That's a thought that'd hamstring St. Vincent de Paul himself, the poor man.

JOSIE (*coming in the door*). Well, isn't he in yet?

WILLIE. No, there's nobody in yet. I thought you were gone.

JOSIE (*coming in and sitting on the bench, her hands in her pockets*). Well, I can change my mind, can't I? Where's Mother?

WILLIE. She's out getting a message.

JOSIE. What's on the plate? (*She looks at it.*) God, what a mess! What's that supposed to be? Hello, Trapper. Yeer back at the oul' Monday-night draughts?

TRAPPER. That was me thought.

JOSIE. That'll be nice. Like old times. Everything in the garden is lovely. How long more will he be? The train must be in. I must get out.

WILLIE. How do I know?

JOSIE. Well, there's no need to be so sharp about it.

WILLIE. Ah, for God's sake, if you are all full of complexes about your father there's no need to take it out on me.

JOSIE. Who's full of complexes? It's you. If I go out and say I'm not waiting you make me feel guilty. If I come back to do the right thing you make me feel guilty.

Well, I came back, didn't I? That should make you happy.

WILLIE. Look, Josie, it doesn't matther a goddam to me what you do. You can go and drown yourself if you like and I won't lose any sleep over it.

TRAPPER. It might be as well for me to depart and come back at a later moment.

WILLIE. Sit down and don't mind her.

JOSIE. How would you feel, Mister O'Flynn, if your father was coming home after doing five years in jail?

TRAPPER. I wouldn't know, Josie agirl. I never knew me father. You understand the implication no doubt, with no aspersions, but if I had a father coming home from jail I imagine it would be betther than having no father in a manner of speaking.

JOSIE. It's all right for men. They don't care. People don't hold it up to them, but they take it out on girls. They pity you. You see them putting their heads together wherever you go, and the fingers pointing at you. You can hide yourself away or you can face up to them, the sly, sleeking things. See, it's all right for Willie. He's stuck in here all day working. He doesn't have to go out into the middle of them, working with them and eating with them and dancing with them.

WILLIE. You must think yourself wonderful important, that you can hold up the movements of a whole town wherever you go so that everyone can down tools to take notice of you. People have more to do than to spend all their waking hours talking about Josie O'Reilly. For God's sake have sense.

TRAPPER. Josie, agirl, don't answer him hastily. In a situation like this spare a thought to the man himself.

Have you no pity for him shut away from freedom for five years, a man like him?

JOSIE. No. That's one bed he made. There was no need for it. It was so needless to kill a man for no reason. If the man had stolen his wife or his money or his soul or anything at all, there might have been a reason.

TRAPPER. In a case like that, me dear, Paddo would have swung. It's because he killed him without a reason that he got only five years. That's the law. Let us accept it and pray for the man's soul.

JOSIE. That's grand, and creep around the corner every time you see Mrs. Green coming down the street. Or not be able to look into Brian Green's eyes.

WILLIE. It's a good job I don't feel that way or I'd never mend Lily's shoes. (*He has them in his hand.*) And charge her for them too.

JOSIE. Lily Green is soft about you. Did you know that?

WILLIE. No.

JOSIE. Well, she is, she is. She always was. They used to write it on the back-door of the Greens' house, in pink chalk, LILY GREEN LOVES HOPPITY O'REILLY.

TRAPPER. Shush, girl!

JOSIE. How does that make you feel? We all know you are soft about Lily Green. The eyes of you when she passes the road. You nearly strain your neck looking after her like a calf. Where does that leave you, Mister Willie O'Reilly? Are you going to court the daughter of the man your father murdered?

WILLIE (*quietly*). I'm going to do better than that, Josie. I'm going to marry her.

JOSIE. You're mad.

26

WILLIE. Not mad. Just lucky. Why do you think I let you get away standing up there trying to put knives into me ? Because of that, sister Josie. You could turn and roast me on a gridiron this minute and I'd only smile at you.

JOSIE. She'd never have you. She's young. She's pretty. You can't dance.

WILLIE. That's right, Josie. Pile it on.

JOSIE (*going over and going down beside him*). Oh, Willie, I'm sorry. I don't know what's wrong with me. I hope Lily Green loves you. I hope she marries you. I hope you will be able to escape. I'm sorry, Willie.

WILLIE. I know you are, Josie. Forget it.

TRAPPER. Well, the ways of women will ever be a wonder.

JOSIE. How can I be such a bitch ? Sometimes I'm nice, Mister O'Flynn. Honest I am. But sometimes I'm terrible. Tell me, Willie. Did you ask her ? When did you ask her ? What did she say ? Tell me ?

WILLIE. Well, actually I don't think I asked her in a way. I'd never have the courage, not me, not good old Hoppity O'Reilly.

JOSIE. Oh, Willie !

WILLIE. She asked me. That's a fact. I'll hold that against her on our golden anniversary.

TRAPPER. There's ambition !

JOSIE. Well, I'm glad. You remember all the fun we used to have long ago, Willie, when we were small. The laughing game we'd play in bed. You know that one, Mister O'Flynn. I say ha, and Willie says ha-ha, and you say ha-ha-ha.

TRAPPER. Ha-ha-ha.

JOSIE. And I say ha-ha-ha-ha and Willie adds another ha and you another to his, and you go on until you have a pain from all the laffin'.

WILLIE. We had good times long ago.

JOSIE (*rising and walking*). And Paddo would come up and pretend to be mad with us and be shouting and he'd end up tickling us or playing the ha-ha game himself. I worshipped Paddo, Mister O'Flynn. I adored my own father. I thought he was God Almighty.

TRAPPER. Everyone remarked it, Josie. It was widely known.

JOSIE. Why did he have to go and do this to me? I'm ashamed of him. He's made us feel so small, so soiled as if we had been rolling in dogs' dung.

TRAPPER. It's not so bad, agirl. It's a lot in the imagination.

JOSIE. No it's not. I know. I feel it. All those years I have felt it. It goes to bed with you, a look that you saw on a face, and you wake up with it in the morning. Wouldn't it have been better to be born a bastard than to be this, the daughter of him?

TRAPPER. You're too hard, Josie, too hard. You are too young, that's your trouble. Wait until you've been out a bit and got a few kicks. Then mebbe you'll think of other people and you'll see that their sores are maybe worse than your own.

JOSIE. I hate facin' him. I hate to meet the look of him. I tried to write to him when he was away but I couldn't do it.

WILLIE. Josie, forget it. It has happened and it will have to be faced. You'll get nowhere in the end, pulling at yourself.

DAYLIA (*coming in the back door closely followed by* BID. *Her face is a little flushed*). Is he here? Has he come? Oh, thank God there's no sign of him. We thought we were late. We were delayed with the message. Thim people. No thought, they haven't. They'd hould you hours, so they would. (*She throws her shawl over the banisters.*) Josie, you're here. Ah, Mister O'Flynn, you in the corner the same as always. Isn't it the blessed thought that brought you? A friend in need.

BID. Him and his oul' draughts. He'd be better off all the years with an oul' woman. That'd crown his king for um.

DAYLIA. Look out the door, Bid, and see is there e'er a sign of them. I had to go for a message for Paddo, Mister O'Flynn. That's what delayed 's. (*She puts a half-dozen bottles of stout in a bag in the cupboard.*) I always used to surprise him on a Monday night when he'd think there wouldn't be a ha'penny in the house. You remember, Mister O'Flynn?

TRAPPER. I do, ma'am, a jewel of a wife you were and no mistake. You made me feel sorry for me single state.

BID. Ther' isn't a sign of a sight of a hair of them. I'll bet Dovetail dragged him into a pub on the way down. If he did, I'll slaughter him.

DAYLIA. The train is in. We saw them coming down from the station in the cars.

TRAPPER. It's possible, ma'am, that Dovetail's Rolls conked out on him. It has been known to happen.

BID. Not at all. Didn't he mend it again before he left? Didn't he, Willie?

WILLIE. That's true. He gave it the paraffin treatment and the toe of the boot and it went like a real motor car.

BID. There !

DAYLIA. Is the kettle boiling ? Oh God, stir up the fire, Josie. What kind angel put his tea out on the plate ? God bless you, Trapper, you should have been a woman.

BID. Isn't ther' enough spinsters in the town without addin' to them ?

DAYLIA. It's wonderful how cheerful I feel now about it all, and half an hour ago I felt like winter. Isn't it true, Bid ?

BID. It's true. You were near walkin' on your heart.

DAYLIA. It's people, Mister O'Flynn. People is so kind. They make the colour of the world, people do. Even the man in the shop where we got the message. He was so kind. He med Bid an' meself have a glass of whiskey to celebrate Paddo comin' home. Didn't he, Bid ?

BID. Ther's no mistake about it. I nearly fell flat with the shock. He probably won't sleep for a week afther it. Whist, I think I hear the sound of Dovetail's car.

WILLIE. That's not his car. It's the stone-crusher at the end of the street.

DAYLIA. Oh, I wish he was here. Josie, girl, you don't know how happy it makes me to see you here to welcome your father home. I was so black because you went away like that. It near med me cry. We're a happy family now again.

JOSIE. Don't kid yourself, Mother. We're a family but we're not happy.

DAYLIA. For the love of God, Josie, don't say anything that'll hurt him. Hasn't he been hurtit enough, I ask you ?

JOSIE. I won't say anything.

30

BID. I knew it. It's Dovetail. Here he is chugging up the street and all the kids in the nation around him. (*Screeching out the door*) Good man, Dovetail! (*Back to them*) It's marvellous how Dovetail always brings home the bacon.

DAYLIA. Is the tea med? Oh, Josie, please make the tea. Here's the canister. I couldn't do it. I have the shakes in me hand. Do I look all right, Willie? (*trying to tidy her grey wispy hair with her hand*). What will he think of the changes in us since he went away?

> *She goes over towards the door.* JOSIE *pours the water into the teapot.*

BID. Them kids! They'll tear the street to pieces.

> *You hear the kids shouting outside the door and* DOVE-TAIL'S *van coming chugging and stopping outside the door. You hear a shrill scream of 'Will we open up now, Dovetail?'* DOVETAIL *answering, 'No, no, not yet, not until ye get the signal. Take it aisy now. Be quiet, will ye! I'll tell ye! I'll tell ye!' We hear the van door banging and then* DOVETAIL *appears at the opening.*

DOVETAIL. Well, have ye got him?

BID. Have we got who?

DOVETAIL. Paddo. Didn't I think he'd be here before me?

DAYLIA. Do you mean to say you haven't him with you?

DOVETAIL. Do you want me to turn out me pockets? I couldn't see him. I searched every inch and corner a the station up to and not including the ladies', and there wasn't a sight of him. All the boys had to go back with their tails between their legs and their speeches stuck in their gullets. They mustn't have let him out at all. Here, ye young bees, keep away from the van. Do you hear me! I'll pulverise a pair of ye.

*He goes out again shouting at the kids.*

BID. Them childer. They haven't an inch a cultivation.

DAYLIA. But what could have happened to him? Why wasn't he on the train?

TRAPPER. Maybe, ma'am, he decided to come be the road.

DAYLIA. What would he do that for and the Government givin' him a special free ticket home for nothin'?

TRAPPER. He had to work five years for it, ma'am.

JOSIE. Well, that's that. I better be on my way.

DAYLIA. But what could have happened to him?

BID. Maybe he wouldn't come back at all to ye, the Lord save us.

DOVETAIL (*coming back in*). So there ye are. I didn't know what to do. I felt like a corpse at a wake. Thim other fellas. Ye'd think it was my fault. It was a poor do. Paddo shouldn't have jilted on his friends like that.

DAYLIA. Did you search the town?

DOVETAIL (*wiping his mouth*). I paid a visit to a few grocery shops on the way back where he might have called but there wasn't a trace of him. Paddo never came home, I tell ye, unless the ground swallowed him up. That's all.

PADDO (*coming in the back door which* DAYLIA *and* BID *left open after them*). No, then, Dovetail, the ground didn't open and swallow him. (*He stands there while they look at him. He is a tall man, wearing a blue suit that seems a little big for him and a collarless striped shirt. His head is bare and shows thick hair, once brown, now raddled with grey. He is carrying a parcel under his arm. His face is strangely pale, an odd paleness that you may also see on the faces of cured lunatics released from asylums. He gives an impression of a man who was immensely strong but who has become bowed, with some of the strength drained out of him.*) Well, Daylia?

DAYLIA (*she is trembling. She is about to sniffle. She raises the end of her apron to her nose*). Oh, Paddo, you have come back.

> *She goes over to him, looking into his face. He puts an arm around her shoulders and puts his face against her hair. Then he raises his face and looks at her.*

PADDO (*freeing himself*). What's it, Daylia? Have you taken to the drink? You smell like an empty whiskey barrel.

DAYLIA (*hand to her mouth*). It was only a little sup, Paddo. Down below, the man in the shop. I was buying a few bottles. He med us celebrate you comin' home, as true as God. Isn't it so, Bid?

BID (*coming over to him and taking his free hand and shaking it*). Paddo Reilly! Paddo Reilly. Me brave boy! Me lovely citizen! Oh God, it's good to see you home.

DOVETAIL (*coming over and shaking the other hand, parcel and all*). Paddo, be the grace of God. Man, but you'd cure an ulcer to see you. Lay it on the plate, man, and call me cuddy. Listen, where were you? Weren't we up there in state? Weren't all the citizens carrying flags to welcome you home? What happened you, man? Where were you? We searched high and low for you.

PADDO. I saw you, Dovetail, so I crossed the line and went out be the bus station.

DOVETAIL. But the celebrations, man. We were laying

them on with a trowel. Such things as we had. Here, hould on. There's part of it outside the door and be-dammed if we'll miss it. (*He goes to the door. Shouts :*) Hey, kids, kids. Let it loose, the man is here. Every one of ye. Now !

> *He guides them with flailing arms. They burst into a shout and then sing a song :*

'Up, Paddo Reilly, he's the champeen of the right :

We'll folly him to battle 'neath the orange, green and white.

Next we'll tackle England and we'll give them hell's delight,

And we'll crown Paddo Reilly King of Ireland.'

DOVETAIL (*looking back over his shoulder for praise*). That's the ticket, men. Give 'm more. Blow the top of yeer lungs this time.

> *They are about to do so, when* PADDO *throws down his parcel and strides to the door. He pushes* DOVETAIL *unceremoniously to one side.*

PADDO (*out at the children*). Go home our that, do ye hear me ! Go home our that or I'll gout and kick a few of the backsides offa ye. Go on now. Get home out of here before I get after ye ! (*He has silenced them. He turns away from them, comes in and bangs the front door closed.*) What kind of a fool do you take me for ? What kind of a spectacle do you want to make of me ? Amn't I shamed enough without you having to make more of it ?

DOVETAIL (*dumbfounded*). But listen, Paddo. It was all meant for the best. We were all glad to see you home. Man, but we missed yeh. There wasn't a sinner in the street that didn't want to welcome you.

PADDO. I don't want to be welcomed. I want to be

forgotten. Has a man no rights at all, that he should be met at the station be every trickey in the town?

DOVETAIL. But, man alive, them weren't trickeys. They were your own. Panther and Munge Arab and God Save the King. Bejay, Paddo, what's come over you? They all love you. They are aristocrats. Doesn't the Mayor himself chat them on the main street when he's givin' them the lend of a few bob?

PADDO. All right, Dovetail. Maybe you meant it for the best. Maybe you saw no harm in it. Let it die now. Go home now, Dovetail, to your own place and leave me in peace with my family.

DOVETAIL. But listen, man . . .

BID (*pulling at his sleeve*). Come on, Dovetail. Give the poor man time to settle down. Leave him in the bosom of his own.

*She hauls him towards the stairs.*

PADDO (*watching them*). Where are ye going?

DOVETAIL. Going home, Paddo. Upstairs. Sure you knew, didn't you, that we rented the top room? We took it three years ago. Daylia said it would help out, the ten bob a week rent. Didn't you know?

PADDO (*looking at* DAYLIA, *who is frightened*). No, I didn't know.

DOVETAIL (*backing up the stairs after* BID, *embarrassed*). Well, that's how it was. Of course. Well, there you are. (*He turns and walks up. He pauses and looks back again.*) How about the bonefire, Paddo? Couldn't we even have the bonefire to-night under the lamp abroad? It's all fixed. (PADDO *just looks at him.*) Well, all right. No bonefire. It will probably rain anyhow.

*He follows her up out of sight.*

PADDO. You could have tould me that, Daylia ? Why didn't you tell me that ?

DAYLIA. Well, I . . . You see, it was hard, Paddo. Things were hard. We had so little. What could we do ?

PADDO. You could have starved before you took the likes of them into our house. That's what you could have done.

JOSIE. It was all right for you. You were getting fed free, weren't you ? It's all right for you to say we could have starved.

PADDO (*as if seeing her for the first time*). Josie ! (*He goes over, stands in front of her.*) You grew big, Josie. You're not much the same at all. Your hair changed colour too. Often and often I wondered what you would be like. You're different. The years make a big difference in young people. You are my daughter, Josie. You have a look of me ? Did you know that ? (*He puts his hands on her shoulders. She pulls away from him, a look of distaste on her face. His jaw muscles harden.*) What's wrong with me ? Have I a disease ?

JOSIE. How would I know what you have ?

PADDO. This is a nice welcome home.

JOSIE. You have a way with welcomes, haven't you ? You doused Dovetail's welcome well. Maybe you did wrong. Dovetail was really pleased to see you home.

PADDO. You feel bad, girl, do you ?

JOSIE. I don't know what way I feel.

PADDO. You could try. This is different. Something is gone wrong here. I saw me coming in the back door and my own family around the fire and I would just sit down and things would be like they were before. We could take up where we left off ?

JOSIE. Well, that's what we're doing, isn't it?

PADDO. No! No! That's not right. I have my wife smelling like a bloody brewery and my house no longer my house with tinkers up in the front room, and you? What have I done to you?

JOSIE. Nothing. Nothing. How do you want me to be? I was young when you went away. You can forget people in five years. Even your own people when you don't see them. You can't stroll back after five years and expect everything to be the same.

PADDO. Is that so, Willie? (*turning to him*).

WILLIE. I'm glad you are home, Paddo.

PADDO. Why can't you look me in the eye, Willie? Are you feeling her way too?

WILLIE (*looking up from* FINNEGAN'S *boot*). I am mending a shoe, Father. If I finish them to-night we will get seven shillings and sixpence. That will provide the dinner for to-morrow.

PADDO. I see.

TRAPPER. Don't push it, Paddo. Take things a biteen easier.

PADDO. How are you, Trapper? I hardly saw you in the corner. You are such a quiet man. Nothing escapes you but you escape everybody. How are you, Trapper?

TRAPPER. I am well, Paddo, and I am glad to see you home.

DAYLIA (*trying desperately to get over her fright and her feeling of despondency*). Paddo, here, I got these for you. (*Taking the bottles of stout from the cupboard.*) I always knew how you love a few bottles of stout on a Monday. See, Paddo, I got them for you, but I wouldn't have got them only for having Dovetail and Bid in the front room.

She paid the rent in advance. Now, Paddo, sure we didn't forget them.

*She is holding the bottles out to him, almost appealingly.*

PADDO. Take them outside in the yard and break the necks and empty them down the sink.

DAYLIA. Paddo, they were for you. Honest to God, I never expected a sup out of them. It was when we were gettin' the message that the man made me take the suppeen of whiskey that you smelled offa my breath.

PADDO. Take them into the yard and empty them down the sink.

DAYLIA (*frightened*). The yard, the sink. All right. I'll . . . I'll do that, Paddo.

PADDO. Where is your thought, woman? You know where I was and why I was there. You know the reason for it, and the first welcome you give me is a blow of it on your breath and bottles of it in your hand. What kind of inhumanity is that, I ask you? What kind of a welcome home is that, I ask you?

DAYLIA. You're right, Paddo. I never thought. Sweet God, if I ever thought! I should be shot, Paddo. I'll empty them into the sink, Paddo, every last drop of them.

*She backs away and then turns out into the back with them.*

WILLIE. She really meant it for the best, you know.

PADDO. I see it all. Ye fester here, the whole lot of ye, thinkin' about yeerselves. About the wrongs I did ye. Did ye ever stop to think a minute about me, meself, and what I was feeling? I can see it in yeer faces. I thought yeer faces would be different. Much different. I wondher should I ever of come home? I wondher would I have

been betther off roamin' the country or stickin' in a cell
and dyin' and rottin' with only false thoughts about the
future that couldn't have been gone sick on me like they
did ?

TRAPPER (*who is playing with the men on the board*). The
game of draughts was invented, Paddo, so that men
could take their minds easy and sit and just think. Sit
down, amac, with your old friend and we'll play a game
of draughts.

PADDO. No ! (*He comes forward and with a sweep of his
hand sends the draughts-board and the men flying all over the
kitchen.*) That was part of it too. You must win at all
costs. You must be a betther man than Trapper O'Flynn.
Don't let Trapper O'Flynn bate you at draughts. Don't
let any man in the world be betther than you at anything.
All that. To be a hayro, in the eyes of the nobodies.
Boast about your strength. About how much porter you
could drink. No, no more of that.

TRAPPER (*going quietly on his knees and picking up the men*).
As you say, Paddo, if that is the way you feel.

PADDO. That's the way. Now you know. (*He goes
over and sits at the table.*) I'll take a sup of tea now, girl, if
it's in it, or did ye wait yeer tea at all for me ? Mebbe
none of ye want to sit at the same table with a criminal.

JOSIE (*her lips tight*). The tea is made. I'll pour it out.
Come over and have your tea, Willie.

> She places the plate of fry in front of her father and then
> fills out the four cups from the teapot. WILLIE *on
> his way over to the table picks up a few men and hands
> them to* TRAPPER. TRAPPER *says* : '*Thank you,
> Willie.*' WILLIE *sits in at the table with his back to
> us. In the silence we hear the sound of a breaking*

> *bottle in the yard.* TRAPPER *finishes gathering his men. He folds up the board and walks tiredly to the door. He opens it and pauses there.*

TRAPPER. You can send for me when you want me, Paddo. I'll come back.

> *Then he goes.* DAYLIA *comes back from the yard.*

DAYLIA. I did it, Paddo. Every last one of them I poured down the sink. Every single drop that was in them.

PADDO. Sit down now and have your tea.

DAYLIA. Yes, Paddo, I will. I'm dyin' for a suppa tay.

> *In order to conform with conventions the curtain may be dropped at this point. It is not necessary, as the action of the play is in one piece, but as you will.*

> DAYLIA *sits opposite* WILLIE, *facing us, and* JOSIE *is sitting facing her father. There is a silence as they eat and sip at their tea. Nobody speaks for a time.* DAYLIA *shows relief in her eyes as* BID *comes down the stairs minus her shawl with a milk-jug in her hand.*

BID. Divil the sup I have above, Daylia astore, and Dovetail bullin' for the milk for his tay. Didn't I mean to get it when we went out for the little message but it ran outa me head like soup offa spoon?

DAYLIA. We have plenty and to spare.

> *She rises and takes her own jug off the table and fills some of it into* BID'S, *who has not come all the way down.*

BID. Just enough to cross a cow, Daylia.

DAYLIA. There.

BID. God bless you and thanks. (DAYLIA *goes back to her place.* BID *gazes down at them. She would feel wrong if she didn't say something.*) Well, yeer the livin' picture of a happy family, God bless ye. Reunited in love, contented and free like the Holy Family itself. (*Since nobody says anything, she goes, trying to excuse her conversation by adding :*) Ah, well, that's the way.

PADDO (*after she has gone*). If they have the big room above, where does Josie and Willie sleep ?

DAYLIA. Well, the way it was, Josie was in with me in our room there athin, until we got ready for you, and so we divided Willie's room in two with a bit of curtain and they bed up there.

PADDO. I had more room than that in jail. They'll have to go.

DAYLIA. It'll be hard on them. Where will they go ? We got kind of used to havin' them around. Dovetail'd give you his last pair a trousers and he can make you laff when your heart is splitting in two. Isn't it so, Willie ?

WILLIE. Dovetail is all right.

PADDO. I got ye somethin' comin' home. 'Twasn't much. (*He rises from the table and picks up the parcel he threw on the floor. He opens it.*) In the town of the jail, it was. It was quare to be in a town. All the people walkin' around the same as if nothing was gone of your life. Sometimes you could hear them at night. Music outside and men going home singing. It was cruel hard to hear them. When the wind was right you could hear the sound of the buses. This is for you (*handing* DAYLIA *a cheap, glittering brooch*).

DAYLIA (*overjoyed principally because good humour seems to be back with him*). Oh, Paddo, it's remarkable beautiful. Wasn't it the good thought that struck you? Janey, I always wanted a brooch like that. (*She puts it in front of her blouse.*) My, don't I look smart, Willie? Law, but you always had the big heart and the thought for people, Paddo.

PADDO. Here, Josie, for you. (*He gives her a colourful head-scarf. She shakes it out.*) It isn't much. I hadn't much money, just a few shillin's that they gev me comin' out.

JOSIE (*surprised and a little touched*). Jay, thanks, Father. It's a beauty. Real silk it nearly is too. You're a good shopper.

PADDO. I got a cobbler's knife for you, Willie. (*Handing it over*) They's real good steel in it, the man says. You can't have enough knives for that leather.

WILLIE. Just the very thing I needed, Paddo. Man, ther's a great edge on it, so there is.

PADDO (*sitting down again*). It's the oney pleasure you get out of being shut up. To be let free again. You have no notion of what it's like. It's like being drunk, so it is, on air. But you feel lost first. Like there was no one at all to take care of you. Like a child you'd be that was let out on its own into a big city for the first time. Listen, you don't know freedom until they take it away from you. A man must ever be free. A man would be betther dead than not to be. If I didn't know I had to suffer for what I done, I couldn't have stuck it. If I had to do it again, I'd take my life.

DAYLIA. Paddo, dear, don't talk like that. It's over now. It's all behind. They's great days ahead. Everything will be bright now, you'll see. I got new sheets on the bed athin and gooses' feathers in the mattress. He'll like a soft bed, I said, afther what he had.

PADDO. You're wrong there, Daylia. Things'll never be the same again. Will things ever be the same again, Josie?

JOSIE. Everythin' changes, I suppose.

PADDO. It's not things that changes, it's people. Think of us five years ago sittin' down at this table. What was it like then, tell me? How different was it then?

JOSIE. We were all younger then.

PADDO. Aye, and we were real people. I saw meself in a shop window comin' home and I had to stand and stare at meself. I'm not half the man I was. I remember damn well what I was like. Then we'd be laffin' now here, the four of us. We'd be laffin' so that we'd be sputterin' crumbs out of our mouths. We'd all be brighter and we'd have betther clothes on us because the money was there. We wouldn't be lookin' like four decayed people with the smell of tribulation rising from us. Well! And it's my fault. Let none of ye think that I don't know that. I know that. When I chopped meself down I chopped the three of ye down with me. That's part of the hard things I thought. I had lots of time to think. I had too much time to think.

DAYLIA. Paddo, for God's sake don't be needlin' yourself. We'll face it now and live it down.

PADDO (*rising*). I'm goin' in to lie down. I have a space in me head with a lot of air whirling around in it.

WILLIE. That's freedom, Father.

PADDO. It might be, Willie. It might be at that. But see the change in me. One time the only time I'd lie down would be when I'd be dead asleep or dead drunk. Now I want to lie down because I don't feel so good.

*He moves towards the passage and the room door.*

DAYLIA (*following him*). I'll stir up the bed for you, Paddo. Will I put a fire in the room ? I'll pull the blind so that the evening light won't blind you.

PADDO. Leave the blind. I want to see the light through four panes of glass. Listen, Willie, and Josie, I'll try and make up for it. I don't know how. I don't even know if I will be able. But I'll try and make up to ye.

*He goes into the room followed by* DAYLIA.

JOSIE. Well, now, what can you make of him ?

WILLIE (*going back to his last*). I don't know. He's a mixed-up man.

JOSIE. You see, he was always that way. One minute you hate him and the next minute he has you hot behind the eyes. Imagine comin' out of jail and goin' straight into a shop to buy a few presents. Imagine that ! (*She is trying the scarf on in front of the mirror.*) That'll give the cats something to read at Mass on Sunday. I could ha' hit him for what he done to Trapper.

WILLIE. Trapper can accept many things.

JOSIE. He med him look so small somehow down on his knees gropin' for the oul' draughts-men. And poor oul' Mother and the smell off her breath. What else had she all the years but a drop of porter to dull her mind a little ? He hadn't to make do. People looked afther him.

WILLIE. Let it go, Josie.

JOSIE. And then he buys us presents. So where are you ? I don't know. Maybe it'll be nice havin' a father again later on, when people have forgotten what happened to him. I'll g'out now and see what me fella thinks of me new scarf.

WILLIE. You're seeing a lot of Manchester.

JOSIE. Well, what of it ?

WILLIE. Nothing. I only passed a remark.

JOSIE. You can pass a remark worse than anyone I ever met. You mind your own business, Willie O'Reilly, and let me mind mine.

WILLIE (*cheerfully*). You can go to hell for all I care. You won't know where you'll end up if you keep after Manchester.

JOSIE. What's wrong with Manchester ? Just because he can afford to own two new suits everybody thinks he has to be crooked. Ye make me sick.

WILLIE. Manchester is as crooked as a ram's horn.

JOSIE. Manchester is put upon. Like me. What does it matter ? I like Manchester. Manchester doesn't give a goddam for anybody in this town. Me choice is limited, isn't it ? It isn't everybody'd be seen around with the daughter of a murderer.

WILLIE. For God's sake don't start that oul' cant again.

JOSIE. Well, it's true. And you leave Manchester alone. I can take care of Manchester.

WILLIE. If you take care of him well enough you might even get him to do a day's work.

JOSIE. To hell with you ! You do many a day's work and where does it get you ? Good-bye. I'm going before I start a row with you and say things that I might be sorry for afterwards. (*She goes to the door.*) And when Manchester owns this town you can come crawling to him looking for a job and I'll get him to give you a kick in the teeth.

*She goes, banging the door.* WILLIE *laughs and continues with his work. Soon* DOVETAIL *comes down the stairs, walking quietly, and wiping crumbs off his mouth.*

DOVETAIL. Is he gone? (*He is whispering hoarsely.*)

WILLIE. He's gone to lie down. He's tired.

DOVETAIL. Tired? He's laid out. I don't know what they did to him down there but they must ha' taken all the mate out 'f 'm. (*He comes over to* WILLIE.) Listen, Willie, you know them things you read in the papers about the weather?

WILLIE. Yes.

DOVETAIL. You know the bad ones they have? A deep depression hoverin' over the West of Ireland? You know that one?

WILLIE. I do.

DOVETAIL. Well, that's me, Willie. I have a depression this minnit that could cover the thirty-two counties. What happened to him, Willie?

WILLIE. I don't know. He's mixed up.

DOVETAIL. Mixed up? Man, he's like a batther pudden. Be rights, Willie, I should ha' been in a circus. Man, I could organise anythin'. Lookit, I had this welcome organised down to the last bottle a stout. And what happens? He blows it up in me dial. I'm depressed, Willie. I am that.

WILLIE. Cheer up, Dovetail, you meant it all for the best.

DOVETAIL. It'd ha' been a whopper, I tell yeh. And that bonefire! Jay, that would ha' been a gift, that bonefire. We could ha' tapped a half barrel around it, so we could, and hump the Guards. I'll never live it down.

WILLIE. People will forget again, Dovetail. They have the habit.

DOVETAIL. They'll all blame me. I was blowin' the whole lot a thum up like a bicycle tyre for the last month. I had them so that they could hardly sleep at night. You'd think that they were waitin' for the Holy Ghost, the way I had them. And now here we are and I have to go and face them. You know something, Willie?

WILLIE. What's that, Dovetail?

DOVETAIL. I'm goin' out now and I'm goin' to get so rotten drunk that I won't know tomorra is Wednesday.

WILLIE. It isn't either, Dovetail, it's Tuesday.

DOVETAIL. Is that so? Well, think of what day I'll think it is when I'm drunk. Here I am, stone-cold sober, and I don't know what day a the week it is. There's one thing certain sure. If ther' was forty-seven different heroes came in at that station above agin, I wouldn't even look at them up on a dray.

WILLIE. Don't get too drunk, Dovetail. It won't fix anything. And himself seems to have taken a turn against the drink too.

DOVETAIL. You see what I mean. What the hell is the prisons comin' to if they even torture a man's thirst out of him? That's a quare hero that won't even knock the top offa pint with his oul' pals.

> *At this point* BID *comes down the stairs with exaggerated care, hushing them with a finger to her lips when the stairs creak under her. She is dragging on her shawl.*

BID. Are you there, Dovetail?

DOVETAIL. No, I'm out in Jerusalem.

BID. He's lost his sense a humour too, Willie. Don't

take it to heart so bad, Dovetail. He'll be different to-morra when he gets used to bein' outa jail. He was so worked up about it, Willie. It was a sad blow to him the way Paddo took it. Where is he?

WILLIE. He's gone to lie down.

BID. Ah, the poor man, he'd go through you to look at him. He took it terrible hard. Why didn't he forget it? Sure, poor oul' Pat Green is in Heaven and betther off than he was. He doesn't have to be workin' like the rest of us.

DOVETAIL. I'll be off. Me heart is as heavy as two hundredweight.

BID. Will I be with you a bit of the road, Dovetail? I have a little message to get down beyant, Willie.

WILLIE. I see, ma'am.

DOVETAIL. Go your own road. This is a night for min only. I have to go down and face the Panther and God Save the King and Munge Arab and explain all to them. Good night, Willie. Try and talk sense to the man. When you see me again stand under the light so that there won't be two of you.

*He goes out the door.*

BID (*looking after him*). Poor oul' Dovetail! Nothin' 'll cheer him up. His heart was set on that bonefire and the childer singin' the song. He was as excited as if he was gettin' married. God, that was a night. Dovetail had so many friends then at it that I didn't get a sight of him until a fortnight after the weddin'. Ah, well, I suppose I betther be goin'.

> *She pauses as she sees the room door opening.* DAYLIA *comes out. She has been doing her best to please. You know it from the careful way she closes the door*

48

*and her tiptoeing into the kitchen, and her coming over and whispering to* BID.

DAYLIA. Thank God, he's stretched out now and when he wakes up he will be a new man.

BID. Praise be. Sure, I'm sure he didn't sleep a proper wink for the whole time.

DAYLIA. You're goin' out, Bid ?

BID. Yes, I was just goin' down the road for a little message. Dovetail deserted me. He went harin' off to his pals. You wouldn't like to come down with me, would you, Daylia ? The walk in the fresh air'll do you good.

DAYLIA (*licking her lips*). I'd love to in a way, Bid, but I'd be afraid he'd wake up and want for something and then there's all the dishes to be washed. They can't be left like that.

BID. Girl, dear, won't we be oney gone for two minutes and what harm can come of them ?

DAYLIA (*looking at* WILLIE). I wonder if I ought to. I'd dearly love a breath a fresh air. Sure it'd do no harm if I went out for a minute, Willie ? Would it, Willie ?

WILLIE (*his head bent over his work*). Please yourself, Mother.

DAYLIA. Wouldn't I be back again while you would be counting up to ten and what loss would be on anything ? I'm so worn out after the day. I really am. All stuffed up inside, I feel, like the middle of pneumonia. Still if he woke up and wanted me and I wasn't here, what would happen ?

BID. Wouldn't he only miss you the more, woman ? That's the way with them. Absence makes the heart grow fonder.

DAYLIA (*taking the plunge, going over for her shawl*). I'll go. Won't I only be a second? What harm can there be in that? Isn't it a great night in a way, if Paddo would only see it that way?

BID. He'll be a different man in the mornin', I tell you. Isn't he like a new calf gettin' the feel of his legs? Sure the man doesn't know where he is, and he says things he shouldn't say and he'd never say the same things if he was in his right mind. Didn't I hear bottles breakin' out in the yard, Daylia?

DAYLIA. It was Paddo. He took a scunner against the drink. He wanted them broke.

BID. God forgive him! We heard a little of it. The door was open. Dovetail was transfixed. I think that's what made him really thirsty.

DAYLIA. Look afther the house so until I come back, Willie. I won't be long. I'll be back before you have stopped looking around you.

*She follows* BID *out of the front door.* WILLIE *stops working, looks after them, shakes his head. Then he rises and goes to the table and gathers up the delf, puts it all into a basin and carries the lot out to the yard. He comes back, takes off the tablecloth and scatters the crumbs into the fire, having put away the bread and butter and sugar. All the time he is whistling the song 'I Know Where I'm Going', smiling as he folds the tablecloth and puts it into the cupboard. He has just done so, and is about to go back to his bench when the* TRAPPER *comes in the door. He is followed by a neat elderly woman wearing a black dress under a black shawl. Her face is thin, her body spare, her deep-sunken eyes kind ; her white hair tied in a bun at the back is a sharp contrast to her black clothes.*

TRAPPER. I have come back, Willie, to turn the other cheek, and to bring a visitor for your father.

WILLIE (*shocked for a little as he looks into her eyes, and then recovering himself*). Won't you take a seat, Mrs. Green? It was nice of you to call.

MRS. GREEN. Thank you. I'm all of a tremble. I was hesitatin' until Mister O'Flynn persuaded me.

TRAPPER. For his own good it will be, you'll see.

MRS. GREEN. So here I am. Where is your father, Willie?

WILLIE. He's back in the room, ma'am. He was lyin' down.

MRS. GREEN. Maybe I betther come back agin?

WILLIE. No, no, sit down. We might as well get it over, I mean it might as well be now as never. Sit down. (*He puts her in a chair near the table.*) Is Lily nearly ready, tell me? Did she tell you that she and me is going out to-night?

MRS. GREEN. She told me. I was very happy, amac. I always have a great regard for you, Willie. She's upstairs now havin' a bath in a basin. She's titavatin' herself.

TRAPPER (*sitting on the stool below the fire*). I have always been agitated at the perfidy of Councils that build houses without baths. What, they say, baths for them bees? Won't they be keepin' the coal in them? That's the oul' propaganda. I wish some of the dirty mullocks had to try and bath theirselves in a basin.

MRS. GREEN. Do you think have I done the right thing, Willie? He'll be pleased to see me, won't he?

TRAPPER. He'll be leppin' out of his shkin.

WILLIE. That's what I'm afraid of. I'll get him for you, and then I'll go up and do meself up.

TRAPPER. Great nights, man. What about Finnegan's shoes ? Have you them done for him ?

WILLIE. I have not. Let him go to hell. I might finish them to-night after I come in.

TRAPPER. That's bad. Finnegan'll die or get to that funeral.

WILLIE. Maybe you'll think Paddo is a bit changed, Mrs. Green. He's not altogether the same man that he was before he went away.

MRS. GREEN. None of us are, Willie. Trapper was telling me about him. He said maybe it would do him good to see me.

TRAPPER. It could be a cure. It's always good to see somebody that's worse off than yourself.

WILLIE. You might be a bad doctor, Trapper.

TRAPPER. I don't think so, Willie. Kill or cure, man. That's the way it is. He has me worried, I'll tell you that. It shouldn't have struck him so hard. Some of us will have to help him.

WILLIE. Even if you get hurt tryin' ?

TRAPPER. Even so.

WILLIE. You're the doctor. Now that you are here, Mrs. Green, have you any objection if I marry your daughter ?

MRS. GREEN. It isn't objection I haven't, Willie, but choice, amac. You don't know Lily. Some time now I knew she had her eye on you. 'God help that boy,' I said. 'She'll take him like a castle.' It will please me, Willie. You are kind. You wouldn't hurt anyone. (*This makes her unhappy as she thinks of what she has said.*

*She looks at him, apprehensively.*) I didn't mean . . .

WILLIE. I know you didn't. That's the only trouble about me and Lily, isn't it? If things crop up?

TRAPPER. Have sense for God's sake. Isn't there too many sensitive people about?

WILLIE. That's right. I'll get him now.

*He goes to the room door, pauses for a moment and goes in.* MRS. GREEN *is nervous.*

MRS. GREEN. Maybe he won't like to see me, Mister O'Flynn? (*She is whispering.*) Maybe the sight of me will bring it all back to him.

TRAPPER. Whist, I tell you it's the best thing you could do for him.

MRS. GREEN. It's the hardest thing I could do, Mister O'Flynn. I can say this to you. Forgive me. I can't forgive him ever for killing Pat.

WILLIE (*coming out of the room*). He'll be with you. He was surprised. I'm off. I'll see you before you go.

*He goes upstairs whistling his tune. Practice has made him good at going up the stairs with his bad leg.*

MRS. GREEN (*still whispering*). Is it an awful thing to say, Mister O'Flynn?

TRAPPER. It's a natural thing for you to say. You have never spoken to him since?

MRS. GREEN. No, Mister O'Flynn. I couldn't bring meself to it. I couldn't.

TRAPPER. I know, I know. Maybe you will be doing yourself some good too. You miss Pat, Mrs. Green.

MRS. GREEN. I do miss him very much, Mister O'Flynn. Nobody will ever know. (*She sits up straight as she hears* PADDO *coming out of the room. His face is very pale. He is wearing a shirt with a heavy brass-buckled belt holding up his trousers. His eyes are glued to hers. She rises as his glance forces her to look at him.*) I came to tell you I'm glad you're home, Mister O'Reilly.

PADDO (*coming over to her slowly*). I don't know what to say.

TRAPPER. Then don't say anything, man, just accept it. You have more friends than you know if you only knew it.

PADDO. You haven't forgiven me, Mrs. Green. No human being could forgive me for what I done. You the least of all, Mrs. Green. Sit down, ma'am.

MRS. GREEN. I do forgive you, Mister O'Reilly. It's a long time ago now, isn't it?

PADDO. It's not to you. I know. It's not a long time to me either. People is surprised when we say that. That's what we share. That thought, that it could have only been last night that I killed your husband.

MRS. GREEN. We will try to forget it, Mister O'Reilly.

PADDO. Oh no, ma'am, we won't. Because that's an impossible thing. I've spent every minute of the time near since it happened wondering what I would say to you the first time I met you. This is the first time I met you. Your husband was one of the finest and most kindly men in the whole town and I had to take him away from you.

MRS. GREEN. We betther try to forget it, Mister O'Reilly.

PADDO. You don't know what you make me feel, seein' you sittin' there under my roof. It is a gesture of God, ma'am, that's all it is. I want to tell you how it happened.

MRS. GREEN. Please, Mister O'Reilly, can't we not talk about it? I thought we wouldn't talk about it, that we'd talk about something else.

PADDO. Listen, ma'am, I owe it to you. For the love of God let me talk to you about it. Nobody else knows what it means. We have the only two hearts in the town that beat in this. It wasn't really me, Paddo O'Reilly, that done it. Some of us are born bad. I'm a bad-born one.

TRAPPER. Man, man, what are you sayin'? You hadn't a bad bone in you ever.

MRS. GREEN. No, no, that's true.

PADDO. That's not true. There's bad in me. I didn't know. What was I? A big strong fella that could jump on to a counter with a hundredweight in each hand. That's what I was. I was a loud-mouthed man. He's a big strong man, they said, with the heart of a child. The heart of a bad child. You know your husband, Mrs. Green. He was a slight man. I could take him in one hand and raise him up to the roof. But he was a better man than I was. He had more brains in the tip of his finger than I had in my whole body. And that was why I killed him.

TRAPPER. Paddo, stop needlin' yourself. Ye were drunk. Everybody in the place was drunk.

MRS. GREEN. It's all over, Mister O'Reilly. It's all over.

PADDO. That's what crucifies me. They should have hung me. I wasn't punished enough for what I done. I was showing them what a great one I was. 'Look at this,' I'd say, clearin' the counter from the stand. Then I took Pat in one hand and raised him off his feet, holding him out from me. I can see his face now. He was smiling at me. 'And yet, Paddo,' he is saying, 'you're twice the man I am and you couldn't add two and two.

That's what he said. 'You couldn't add two and two.'

TRAPPER. He always had a great head for sums, Pat had.

PADDO. They brought out the board, the black one they had, and a piece of chalk. And we matched drink with drink. It was whiskey. Man for man. The stupidity of it! Great God, what sort of an animal was I at all? He'd shout out a sum and he'd write it down and I'd write it down and every time he'd be there standin' back while I was stumped. He had the good head. I had the bad head. What possessed us at all? What was it all about? It was all about nothing. And the figures danced there under me fingers and I couldn't see them. They wavered and wavered and I hit him. That's what they tell me. I don't remember. I don't remember at all. I can't remember at all. But why did I hit him? Because he punctured me, Mrs. Green. Because he was a better man than I was. It wasn't the drink. How could it be the drink? That's only an excuse for nothing. Nothing at all. But I saw him on the floor and his hat off and there was blood at the side of his mouth. There was somebody roarin'. That was me. But he was peaceful. He was shockin' peaceful there with his hair in the sawdust.

MRS. GREEN. For God's sake, Mister O'Reilly, leave me alone, can't you? Let him rest, can't you? I didn't come for you to bring him up out of the grave for me. Stop it now.

PADDO (*wiping his forehead*). I'm sorry. I had to say it. That's the picture I take to bed with me every night I go to sleep.

MRS. GREEN. Yes, but I have a different one, Mister O'Reilly. I have a different one.

PADDO. I know. I know, honest to God I know. I thought of you often at home in your room below waitin' for him to come home. And how he came home to you. I saw that too.

MRS. GREEN. Mister O'Reilly, I must go home (*rising*).

PADDO. I don't blame you, ma'am. I don't know how you could have come near me. I'd ha' sooner walk in the pludder of a pighouse than come near me.

MRS. GREEN (*sitting again*). But that's not it, Mister O'Reilly. I don't feel that way about you. It's just that Pat to me was Pat. And even if everybody has forgotten him, his own childer even, he is alive to me. I don't want to hear you talking about him dead, Mister O'Reilly. That's what I mean. I don't mean that I can't stand with you because you took him away.

TRAPPER (*rising*). I think we bether go, ma'am. This is doing nobody any good.

PADDO. Do go, now, let ye. I'm sorry. I don't know what I'm sayin' sometimes. I hope I didn't hurt you, ma'am.

MRS. GREEN. I'm gone past being hurtit now, Mister O'Reilly. There's not much can hurt me any more. I'm glad you're home. Your family needs you at home. They had hard times without you. Times will be bether now. Times will be bether for all of us. God is good.

PADDO. God is just, ma'am. God will look after people like myself.

MRS. GREEN. We bether go, Mister O'Flynn. Everything I say now is going wrong.

*She goes towards the door.*

TRAPPER. Right, ma'am. I tell you something, Paddo. You want to get a grip on yourself. No man minds a fella

57                                                              E

hurting himself, but sometimes when a fella is hurting himself he reaches out and hurts everyone else that's near him. That's bad. Think of all the good things there are for you and stop broodin' on all the bad things.

PADDO. I'll tell you this, ma'am, never till the day I die will a drop of drink cross my lips. If it hadn't been for that nothing might ever have happened. We could be talkin' together now like two ordinary people, friendly, instead of standing here with a terrible wall of blood between us.

MRS. GREEN. Things will be betther to-morra, Mister O'Reilly. You'll feel betther to-morra.

*She goes out quickly.*

PADDO. She hates me. And who can blame her? She hates the very sight of me, and who can blame her?

TRAPPER. Paddo, you're in a mess. You're in a bigger mess now than ever you were in your life. The trouble about big fellas like you is when you start thinkin' when you weren't made for thinkin'. Stop thinkin', for the love of God, and become what you were when we all knew you. Now none of us know you. (*He follows her.* PADDO *stands looking after them for a time. Then he sits down, buries his head in his hands. He looks around, gets up and goes over to the stairs and shouts*) Willie! Hey, Willie!

> *He walks back to the fire and pokes at it, then goes over to the picture of himself and* DAYLIA *on the wall and stands looking at it.*

WILLIE (*coming half-way down, drying his face on a towel*). Well, what is it?

PADDO. Where's Josie? Where's your mother? Where's everyone?

WILLIE. They're out.

PADDO. Out! Out! What kind of inhuman beings are they at all? Couldn't they stay an hour in the house the first night I am home?

WILLIE. You were supposed to be sleeping. What would they do? Stick around and listen to your sleeping?

PADDO. It's time I came home. This house is gone to hell since I left it. Is this true about Josie goin' around with this Monaghan thing?

WILLIE. You ask Josie that.

PADDO. Why didn't ye stop her? Why did you let her get caught up with bad ones like that?

WILLIE. Are you sure he's bad?

PADDO. The bad drop was always in him. It's men like him jails were built for. His father before him was as bad as him. Even far away as I was I knew what was going on in this town. That's the worst part of it when they take five years out of your life. It's what happens to your family (*walking over to the fire*). If I had been here things would be different. Ye would have grown different.

WILLIE. Maybe we wouldn't.

PADDO. You're agin me too, aren't you? What have I done apart from the main thing that I have to try and fight my way back into ye? I'm still your father. I'm still the same inside no matter what the outside of me has done.

WILLIE. Maybe you're not the same inside.

PADDO. What do you mean by that?

WILLIE (*coming down a little*). What do I mean? I was listening to you talking to Mrs. Green. Would the Paddo of five years ago have been the same cruel man that was talkin' to that woman?

PADDO. I said nothin' cruel to her.

WILLIE. That's the worst of it. You don't even see it. You put a rusty knife in her guts and turned it. That's all you done.

PADDO. You don't understand. You're too young to understand. How can I make ye understand? It's you that can't see what is wrong. Look at your mother. What happened to her? Where is she now? Out boozin' I'll be bound, with that withered guzzler from upstairs. What happened your mother in the years? Am I to blame for that? She was a decent hard-workin' woman when I left her. Look at her now, with the eyes in her bloodshot and a tremble in her hand. Would that have happened if I was here? Am I to blame for the unhappy house that ye have turned into?

WILLIE. Listen, Paddo, it wasn't an unhappy house. You are wrong. It was a happy house. If you left now and went away it would still be a happy house.

PADDO. I'll make up for it. I'll bring ye back. I'll bring ye back, be the Almighty God, if I have to drive ye with leather.

WILLIE. You will be wrong again, Paddo. We are too set now to be driven. Don't make a mistake there.

PADDO. Am I mad? Am I standin' here and have me own son, a half man, talking to me like that?

WILLIE. Remember who made me a half man. I'm my father's son. Remember that, Paddo. This house was all right, and I'm tellin' you now to leave it as it was and if you don't like it you can leave it to itself. You destroyed us, but we built oursel' back into what we are now, however poor, and nothing is going to change that. If my mother likes a bottle of stout, what's wrong with that ? What made her like it ? If Josie likes Manchester Monaghan, what's wrong with that ? It's her life. I like my life. You fight your own corner, but if you try to rattle us you are going to be up against it. I'm tellin' you that.

PADDO. Thank God for the patience of prison. That's all I can say. If it wasn't for that I'd have you reelin' across the kitchen with a blow in the puss.

WILLIE. You could try that too. You often did it. But you won't do it again — not any more, Paddo. You'll get as good as you give.

PADDO (*approaching him appealingly*). Willie, what's wrong with us ? What started this ? I had no notion that we would be talkin' like this.

WILLIE. I hadn't either, Father. I had a hard time too while you were away. I worked long hours to keep a roof over our heads. But I did it and it rarely leaked. Now I can't let you fault it. And you can't build a new one on top of it. You'll have to become a part of it or we'll all have to find new nests.

PADDO. What do you want me to do, Willie ?

WILLIE. I don't know. Just leave us alone. It would be a good idea to stop thinking of yourself for a while.

PADDO. I've had long practice at that, Willie.

WILLIE. Well, I don't mean that, it's just . . . well, that's what it boils down to, leave us alone.

PADDO. Willie, you bether go upstairs and finish your washin'. Because I think you stopped growing up the day I left ye. You have nothin' in your head but air. What are you trying to do ? Is it to dominate me you want ? What made you a philosopher ? You're tellin' me out of your own mouth the wrong things that

61

happened ye while I was away. I'm telling you this now, Willie, there's goin' to be a cure of it. Dovetail and his wife will be out of this house to-morra mornin' on the back of their necks if they don't go peaceful. That'll cure your mother. I'll cure Josie and I'll cure you.

WILLIE. It's useless talkin' to you (*going back upstairs*). You're goin' to strike around you like a wounded tiger. That's what they do. They're animals with oney instinct. You're supposed to have brains like a human being. You ought to use them.

PADDO. Get upstairs, Willie, before I lose me temper. I'm tellin' you to go upstairs before I lose me temper.

WILLIE (*on the way up*). I'm goin' upstairs because I want to finish washing and get dressed, not because you are going to lose your temper. Remember that, Paddo. I don't give a goddam about your temper. I have one too. You lose yours and I'll lose mine and then I'll show you the inheritance you handed on to me.

> *He goes out of sight.* PADDO *stands looking after him, his hands gripping the banisters. He is pale with suppressed anger. He hits a clenched fist on the knob of the banisters. The front door opens and* LILY *comes in. She has changed into a light-coloured frock over which she is wearing a coat. She is obviously all out. You can nearly get the scent of the soap and the perfume from her. She stands inside the door. She looks at him. Her eyes are bright.*

LILY. Hello, Mister O'Reilly. (*He looks at her blankly.*) Don't you remember me? You are welcome home.

PADDO. No, agirl, I'm sorry. I don't remember you. You would have been small when I left home.

LILY. Faith, I wasn't so small at all. I'm Lily Green.

PADDO. Lily . . . Green.

LILY. Yes. That's right.

PADDO. I see, agirl. (*He turns away towards the fire. He sits on the bench. His head drops in his hands. Then he raises it.*) There's great charity in the Greens. Have you come to forgive me too?

LILY. No, Mister O'Reilly. I've come for Willie. We're going out. Where is he?

PADDO. He's upstairs. I wondered why he was washing. Now I know. You are a very pretty girl, Lily Green.

LILY. I wondered where Willie got the soft tongue. Now I know.

PADDO. You knew me before I went away. Have I changed much in your eyes?

LILY (*looking at him critically*). Yes. Your hair is grey and your face is lined and you don't seem to be as big a man as I remember you. I used to think you were a proper giant. But I was young then. Isn't it quare the way things get smaller when you get older?

PADDO. That's a quare thing right enough. Are you and Willie friends, tell me?

LILY. Indeed we're more than friends. We're going to be very closely related. Willie and me is going to be married.

PADDO. What did you say?

LILY. It's oney to-night, just before you came, that he asked me. Of course we knew for ages but we never kind of talked about it until to-night.

PADDO. Do you know what you are saying?

LILY. Indeed I do. Well I know. Why? What's wrong with it?

PADDO. And you know who I am?

LILY. Sure I do. You are Willie's father.

PADDO (*standing*). I know! I know! But I'm more than that. I'm the man . . .

LILY (*interrupting impatiently*). I know, you're the man that killed me father. What's that got to do with Willie and me?

PADDO. Great God, how hard young people can be and how aisy they forget! Does your mother know that you and Willie are great?

LILY. Of course she does.

PADDO. And does she agree to it?

LILY. Why wouldn't she? What's wrong with you, Mister O'Reilly?

PADDO. It's not what's wrong with *me*, but what's wrong with you. Does your dead father matther so little to you that you'd turn around and marry the son of the man that killed him?

LILY. Mister O'Reilly, I think you ought to let my dead father rest.

PADDO. How in the name of the good God can the man rest and you talking of doin' what you're goin' to do?

LILY. My father was a quiet man. We never did anything to hurt him. He never did anything to hurt us. My mother came to see you to welcome you home. It didn't do her any good, Mister O'Reilly. You had her cryin' her heart out. What were you sayin' to her?

PADDO. That's between the two of us. But this is different. Listen, girl, if you can't see it yourself, I'll have to tell it to you. This. You cannot marry Willie. All the dacency in the world wouldn't let ye do it. You won't marry Willie, agirl. Because I won't let you.

LILY. How can you stop us, Mister O'Reilly? We are both old enough to know our own minds. Has Willie changed his? Has Willie said he wouldn't marry me?

PADDO. If he hasn't I'll say it for him. Over my dead body ye'll marry. Merciful Father, what's got into ye? Can't ye see the future? Can't ye hear what people will say? Can't ye see the day that ye will have to tell yeer children the story of yeer beginnings? How much agony can a man stand? Do ye want to pile on more agony into me mind until I go out of my head?

LILY. I'm sorry for you, Mister O'Reilly, but you can't stop us doing what we were made to do.

PADDO. I'll stop ye. No priest in the town would dare to marry ye. I'd cry ye from the steps of the altar if I had to.

LILY. It's no good, Mister O'Reilly. If we can't get a priest to marry us we'll marry anyhow. This is past you, Mister O'Reilly. I'm sorry for you. I thought you would be different. But you're worse than I thought.

PADDO. You can't see it! All right. You won't. Go home now, girl, and put the whole thing out of your head.

LILY. Would you call Willie down now, I want to see him?

PADDO. I won't call Willie down. You will leave this house now, agirl, and as long as I am here you will never meet under my roof. You understand that?

LILY. Frankly, Mister O'Reilly, I don't. All I can see is that you hurt us once very much and that you seem to want to keep on hurting us.

PADDO. Don't say that! That's not true. How can I make you see?

LILY. We're lookin' through different glasses. Very well. You won't call Willie. I could call him but I won't. I'll go, Mister O'Reilly, out of your house like you told me (*she goes to the door*), but I'll come back again for Willie. He needn't come with me if he doesn't like. But he will. You'll see. And he'll stay with me. Nobody is going to spoil our lives, Mister O'Reilly. Nobody at all.

*She goes.*

PADDO (*following after her*). Come back, do you hear? Come back!

> *But she is gone. He can't follow her into the street. As he stands there at the door we hear* WILLIE *whistling upstairs. He is whistling 'I Know Where I'm Going'.* PADDO *listens for a while. Then he walks over to the picture of the Sacred Heart. He gets on his knees in front of it and prays silently and violently, hitting his breast three times. Then he rises, looks around him, goes over to the picture of himself and* DAYLIA, *and with his teeth clenched raises his hand to it and turns it so that it faces the wall and presents a cobwebbed back to our view. Then he goes into his room and closes the door. The door is barely closed when the front door opens and* JOSIE *comes in. She looks around, turns and speaks back over her shoulder.*

JOSIE. There's nobody here, but you can come in anyway.

> *She comes in towards the fire, taking the scarf from her head and swinging it in her hand. She is followed by a tall thin young man. He is very well dressed in a grey pin-stripe suit with the stripe a little too wide*

66

*for decency. A pink shirt and a blue tie provide a startling contrast to the view. He is sallow-complexioned, handsome, with a suspicion of a moustache, and his hair is stuck to his skull with oil. His eyes are keen. He takes in the place deliberately.*

THE MAN. So this is the shack. Not bad!

JOSIE. If I knew you were going to force your way into it, we'd ha' had the Chinese carpet cleaned.

THE MAN (*sitting at* WILLIE's *bench and idly fingering the tools*). It was far away from Chinese carpets you were dragged up.

JOSIE. Now you seen it, Manchester, let's get goin'.

MANCHESTER. I wanted to see your father too, don't forget.

JOSIE. But why?

MANCHESTER. Why? Why? Why? How is it that everybody else can just do things and everything I do I have to give a blue-print for it?

JOSIE. That's your own fault. Nobody built your reputation but yourself.

MANCHESTER. It's envy, that's what it is. This whole town is a sea of envy. Just because a fella can buy a few suits and not be goin' around with the backside out of his britches there must be somethin' wrong with him.

JOSIE. All the town wants is to see you doing a single day's work and they'll be happy.

MANCHESTER. They'll have long grey whiskers before they see that. I work harder than any of them, so I do. Where do you think I get me livin'?

JOSIE. I wish I knew. I'd give up workin' meself.

MANCHESTER. All right. You go along with them too. Ye make me sick. It's got to the point now, that if a mother even sees me talkin' to her daughter she starts screamin' for an affiliation order. Honest to God, Josie, I'm serious, I tell you. I like you very much. I keep tellin' you that. Let your guard down a bit, can't you? You're all armoured like a tank. Every time I come out with you I have to think of taking a seventy-five-pounder gun.

JOSIE. Is that what you want me father for, to borrow a bazooka?

MANCHESTER. Ach, be serious, can't you?

JOSIE. All right, Manchester, I'll be serious. I like you too. I think you're very nice. I think it's great fun being with you, but I don't know if you are as black as you are painted. What do you want me to do, take you at your face value and join the affiliation order queue? You have a bad reputation. You know that. So far I don't know whether it's earned or not. You have a dangerous way with you and I'm only a poor weak woman.

MANCHESTER. May the Lord God preserve us all from poor weak women.

JOSIE. You don't trust me, Manchester.

MANCHESTER. If I gave you the same amount of trust that you give me you could hide it in a flea's ear. Damn it, Josie, I thought you had sense. What's a reputation? It's like the froth on the top of a pint. There's nothing to it. It suits me to have a reputation. If I was guilty of all the girls I'm down for, I'd want to have the stamina of a Shorthorn bull. (JOSIE *laughs*.) Well, it's true. For the love of God don't believe all you hear. It's the first time in me life that I have felt sorry for a reputation. You know how it is with young fellas. Every girl they go out

with when they're young they have to come back to the
chaps and wink the eye and use the elbow and say, Boy,
was she hot stuff! It's all guff, I tell you. It's really a
sign of great purity. (JOSIE *laughs again*.) Well, as long
as I can be your comic. Do you believe that? As true
as I'm here in this house, I'm innocent of ninety-nine per
cent of what I'm put down for.

JOSIE. And who was Miss One Per Cent?

MANCHESTER. She was a girl like you, Josie. She was
a nice girl. I liked her. But she hadn't courage either.
She could never get herself to the point of believing that
every word out of me mouth wasn't a lie. I had to meet
her around back-alleys and side-roads. She was afraid
what her parents would say if she was seen with me. I
played with her until I got sick of the sliding. I'm not a
dirty tom-cat. I'm a nice clean-livin' fella and I like you
and I want to see your father, and when I see him I'm
goin' to face up to him and I'm goin' to say, 'Please,
Mister O'Reilly, do you mind if I marry your daughter?'

JOSIE. What?

MANCHESTER (*rising and coming over towards her*). Yes,
Josie, I like you that much, believe me. It feels good to
me to be walking beside you, looking into shop windows,
thinking of a small, nice, snug Council house up in
Bohermore with me out in the spring evening with me
coat off digging the spuds.

> *He is close to her, his hands on her arms, his face close
> to hers.* JOSIE *is fascinated.*

JOSIE. It's in the autumn you dig the spuds.

MANCHESTER. Well, in the autumn. And I can see you
comin' out in your nice neat apron callin' me into the
house for a feed of crubeens and bacon, and before we go

in we'll tiptoe over to the grand shiny new pram with the cream lace cover on it and we'll peep in at the young Monaghan suckin' his thumb and his blue eyes the colour of the clear sky. Oh God, that'll be something.

> *He is close, very close to her now, his hands stealing up her back, caressing her shoulders. He is almost about to kiss her when she breaks away and gets to the other side of him.*

JOSIE (*a little breathlessly*). Here now, hold on a minute. You nearly had me there, Manchester. Diggin' spuds in the spring. What kind of an eejit do you take me for?

MANCHESTER. What the hell does it matter about the spuds. I meant all the rest.

JOSIE. Looking into shop windows. You know what I see when I think of that and I out here away from you, I think of you looking at the nice new goods in the windows and working out how you can get your hands on them.

MANCHESTER. Josie, be reasonable.

JOSIE. And where do we get the nice new pram with the cream covering on it, I'd like to know? Do we get it Cathleen Mavourneen or do you whip it out of the factory?

MANCHESTER (*deeply hurt, apparently, and going to pass her by*). All right, if you take me for such a goddammed monster there's nothing more that we can say. (*He goes to the door.*) Good night, Josie, and good-bye.

JOSIE (*stopping him, her hand on his arm*). Really, Manchester, tell me the truth. Was the whole lot of them speeches galoo or did you mean even one item on the programme? Tell me, honestly.

MANCHESTER. What's the use of telling you honestly when you think I'm drippin' lies like a burst pipe?

JOSIE (*coaxingly*). Ah, but really, Manchester.

MANCHESTER. Of course I meant them, every single one of them. What do you want me to do, cut me throat and swear it with me dyin' breath?

JOSIE. No, just say one or two of them over again, until I see you have them off by heart.

MANCHESTER (*pulling away to go*). Ah, to hell with you.

JOSIE (*holding on to him*). No, no, Manchester, I'm only jokin'. What about all the other things? What about the way you make your livin'? How about what would happen if somebody offered you a nice honest job?

MANCHESTER (*bitterly*). There's the women now for you. A man makes a major blunder impelled by true love and he ends up down at the Docks covered all over in coal-dust at fifteen bob a day.

JOSIE (*her arms around his neck*). Would you, Manchester, would you for me make the final sacrifice, even if it was down at the Docks, would you?

MANCHESTER (*under a bit of a spell now in his turn*). Well, I . . . might.

JOSIE. Manchester, I don't think you are as black as you are painted.

> *She kisses him slowly. He reacts pretty well, and they are there locked in this close embrace when* PADDO *comes out of the room. He stands and stares at them.* MANCHESTER *is the first to see him, raising his head. The look on his face of a cat after drinking a saucer of cream changes slowly to the sort of guarded look of good humour which is* MANCHESTER'S *habitual disguise. He beams.*

MANCHESTER. Well, Mister O'Reilly, I don't have to say any more, do I? I could have med a speech for two hours and couldn't have tould you as much as you seen.

JOSIE *turns around. She is not embarrassed.*

JOSIE. Hello, Paddo. Manchester wanted to see you, so I brung him.

PADDO. Get out of here, Monaghan.

MANCHESTER. Here, hold on; I came to act the part of the good neighbour. You don't know me well. I have a lotta feelers out in the town. So when I knew you were back and me having a feeling for Josie the way I have, I knew you'd want a job of work, and I'm the man that can get you a job.

PADDO. You'd be betther employed from what I hear gettin' a job for yourself.

JOSIE (*getting a little angry*). Listen, Paddo, there's no need to be rude to Manchester. He kem here full of good-will.

PADDO. Well, he can take his good-will with him and get out of here before I kick him out.

MANCHESTER (*approaching him soothingly*). Now listen here, Paddo.

PADDO. Mister O'Reilly to you. Because I come out of jail is no reason for trickeys like you to be callin' me be me first name.

MANCHESTER (*becoming annoyed*). Right you are, your Highness, if that's the way you feel, condemnin' a man before you know whether he's your betther.

JOSIE. Don't mind him, Manchester. Let him go to hell. Come on and get out of here. If I thought you'd have been insulted the minute you put your foot inside the door, I'd ha' died before I let you come.

MANCHESTER. Now, listen, maybe we're all gettin' a bit heated over nothin'.

PADDO. Get out of here and stay out of here, and keep away from my daughter or I'll make you sorry.

MANCHESTER. All right. You've made yourself clear. Come on, Josie.

PADDO (*moving towards them*). She's not going with you. She's goin' to stay here where she is.

JOSIE. And who's going to stop me goin' out with him?

PADDO. You'll stay where you are.

JOSIE (*turning to go*). Come on, Manchester. We betther go before I say something I'll be sorry for.

*She takes his arm and is about to go out with him. PADDO moves to them quickly and angrily. He catches her free arm and pulls and she comes back behind him, slithering. She almost falls. She ends up over near the fireplace.* PADDO *faces* MANCHESTER. MANCHESTER *is surprised.*

PADDO. Do you have to go now, or do I put you? I tell you now, Monaghan, I'm coming to the end of me tether.

MANCHESTER. Well . . . I don't see any reason to mix it with a murderer.

JOSIE. Manchester, don't go. Don't give in to him.

PADDO. Get out now, fast, Monaghan, before me temper goes on me.

MANCHESTER. I'm going now because I'm mixed up. I don't know how to handle you, Paddo, but I will. I'll be back.

*He retreats out of the door.* PADDO *follows him up, closes the door after him and clicks the bolt on it. Then he turns back to her.*

PADDO. What do you mean goin' about with a thing like that? What do you mean?

JOSIE. What do you mean pushin' me about the kitchen as if you were my father?

PADDO. I am your father.

JOSIE. Who told you? Isn't it a bit late for you to think it? You should have thought of it years ago before you batthered a man to death that wasn't half your size. That's when you should have thought it.

PADDO. Shut your mouth.

JOSIE. I will not shut me mouth. Who the hell do you think you are? Do you think you can spend five years in a jail, disgracin' the lot of us to death, and then when we have got over a bit of the shame that you come back and tell us you're our father? You're no father of mine, and stand out of the way now. I'm goin' out to Manchester Monaghan and neither you nor anyone else is goin' to stop me.

PADDO. You'll stay in now to-night and you'll go up to your room and you'll go to bed, and if I ever catch you with that scab again I'll take the strap to you. Do you hear that?

JOSIE. Poor Paddo! You are too late now. You are a few years too late. You should have thought of being a father before you struck the blows.

PADDO. I'll tame you. I'll teach you out of your dirty ways if I have to leave you black and blue. Do you hear that? You can taunt me away. You can throw me sins into me face five times a night, but I know what I have to do and I'll do it. I'll wipe the evil years out of ye.

JOSIE. You are too late, Paddo. You aren't fit to black Manchester's boots, so you are not. The dirtiest bowsey in the town has it over on you because nobody can ever call them with the disease you have, the prison pus.

PADDO. Get up to your room!

JOSIE. You have it, Paddo. It's workin' up in you. You'll hit every one of us now until it's driven out of your body. You'll make every one of us suffer now, won't you, until the last drop of pus is squeezed out of you?

PADDO. Get up to your room.

JOSIE. I will not. I'm going out. I'm going out to Manchester.

PADDO. For the last time, go up to your room.

JOSIE. I'm going out to Manchester. Manchester is a betther man than you, Paddo. He smells clean. He has good in him. He doesn't smell of the smell that is off you. Five years of rot.

PADDO (*losing control of himself*). Shut up. You . . . you . . . you don't know what you are talking about, you little slut. That's what has become of you. A little slut. What were you when I went away? A clean little girl, clean, clean and decent, and I come out and see you loose, loose and dirty, stretching your body in that fella's arms.

JOSIE (*passing him by and going to the door*). I'm going out to Manchester.

*She is pulling at the bolt.*

PADDO (*striding for her and reaching for the buckle of his belt with one hand. He frees it practisedly and grabs her shoulder with the other*). I have to teach you. I can do nothing but teach you.

JOSIE. Lea' me alone. Take your dirty hands offa me.

PADDO. Ye won't be taught except the hard way. Me heart was soft for ye but it did no good. God put a burden on me to take care of ye. I will take care of ye.

JOSIE. Let me alone. Let me alone!

*She struggles in his grasp. The coat slips from one
shoulder and his strong hand tears the frock at her
neck. Then he raises the strap high and brings it
down on her.*

PADDO. I'll bring ye back. I'll tear the five years of
evil out of ye.

JOSIE *tries to dodge the blows. His grasping hand
tears the frock further until one shoulder is disclosed.
She screams loud and clear. He raises the strap
again, forcing her to her knees. If you do not wish to
see further, you may drop the curtain.*

*Hearing* JOSIE'S *screams* WILLIE *has come down from
upstairs. He has put on a white shirt, is wearing the
trousers and waistcoat of a nice new blue suit. The
tie is hanging around his neck as he was fixing it when
he heard her calling. He has come down, grabbed the
knife his father presented him with from the bench
in passing, freed his father's grasp on his sister and
pushed him away from her. So now you see him
facing his father, the knife clenched in his hand. He
doesn't hold it as if he was going to use it, just the way
you would grab up something because it is a weapon.*

PADDO. Get out of the way now, I tell you, she has
more coming to her.

WILLIE. You've done enough now. You'll have to
tackle me now, before you get at her.

PADDO. Get out of the way, I tell you.

WILLIE. No, and if you have sense you will. I knew this was coming. I had the feeling from the way you were carrying on. Get up off the floor, Josie, and go wherever you want. (*She gets to her feet slowly while the two face one another.* PADDO *is on the point of using the buckle on his son, but* WILLIE *has a determined look in his face and the light is glinting off the new steel of the knife.*) It's yours. It's your gift, Paddo, and if you hit me, I'll give it back to you. I swear my oath I'll give it back to you.

JOSIE. Go on, Willie, give it to him. Dig it to the maker's name in him !

WILLIE. Cool off now, Josie. Why did he do it ?

JOSIE. Because he's a savage. Because Manchester was here. That's funny. You know what Manchester wanted, Willie ? He wanted to ask your man if he could marry me. Is that a joke ? He didn't get time to open his gob before he run him, and then went for me because I wanted to go with him.

PADDO. You stupid. Do you think the likes of him would want to marry you ? Have you any sense in your head ? You'll get it, my girl, you'll get it before I'm done with you.

WILLIE. Go on out to Manchester now if you want to, Josie. Go wherever you like now, Josie.

PADDO. She's not puttin' a foot outside that door.

WILLIE. Listen, Paddo, it won't work. If you stop her you'll have to stop me first. You can work it out for yourself. I say she goes. You say she stays. It'll have to be a trial, Paddo, and she'll be gone anyhow before it's decided. So go now, Josie, when I tell you.

PADDO *can't decide as she moves towards the door, pulling her dress together. He looks closely at* WILLIE. WILLIE'S *gaze doesn't waver. Finally* PADDO *starts to buckle on his belt.*

JOSIE (*at the door*). You'll be the sorry man. You will that. Manchester is in earnest. Manchester will get you when I tell him what you done with me. I'll find Manchester, and I'll sleep with him down in the Baulks. I'll sleep with him in a stable or up in the Square. I'll do everything I can with him. I'll show you in reality what your dirty mind was playin' with. Good-bye, Father. You'll never see me again while I have a pair of eyes, and this house will never see me until you are out of it.

 *She goes.*

PADDO. You hear that! That was my little girl. Before I went away at this hour of the night she'd be down on her knees sayin' God bless Mammy and God bless Daddy, and now you hear the filth that is pouring out of her. In five years. Tell me this, Willie, haven't you something to answer for now?

WILLIE. I have many a thing to answer for. But you have to answer for her. Don't saddle me with your sins, Paddo.

PADDO. I'm goin' down for your mother. Where is she? What pub does she do her drinkin'?

WILLIE. How do I know. Maybe she's not in a pub. Maybe she's in the chapel sayin' her prayers.

PADDO. I'll find her. That young Green one was here. Did you know that?

WILLIE. I heard her talking.

PADDO (*moving to the room for his coat. As he goes in*). Did you hear me talking to her, Willie?

WILLIE. I did not. She is well able to take care of herself.

PADDO. Well, I told her something. (*He comes out. He is pulling on his coat.*) What possessed you to be goin' after her? Have you no sense of decency? I told her.

WILLIE. I'll bet you told her.

PADDO. I told her. I'll folly ye to the altar. Remember that, Willie. That's one thing that's not goin' to happen as long as I have a drop of blood in me veins.

WILLIE. You can do what you like, Paddo. You can let your twisted mind work whatever way it wants. We've gone past you.

PADDO. You think that. I'll reduce you, Willie. I'll reduce your arrogance for you. I'll cut you down to your proper size.

WILLIE. You'll have to work fast, Paddo. You'll have to work very fast, or you'll be left alone. I'd go into a church meself if I was you, Paddo, and I'd pray a bit and I'd think a bit.

PADDO. Ye had five free years to pray, but ye didn't do it.

*He turns to go out by the back door.*

WILLIE. Look, Paddo, go easy with my mother, I'm tellin' you.

PADDO. She's my wife, Willie. She's the only thing in the world I have left with me. Now I know that. I'll look afther her, don't you fret.

*He goes.* WILLIE *stands a time looking after him, then he hears the knock on the front door. He goes to it, opens it, and* LILY *comes in. He closes the door after her.*

WILLIE. There was a time when that front door was never shut. Now it has to be shut while we cringe behind its cover. Are all the neighbours out?

LILY. Every single one of them. Every door has a woman with her arms folded and her neck stretched talking to the next one. It was Josie roaring.

WILLIE. You heard that?

LILY. If you were a Chinese you would have heard it.

WILLIE. It's a quick change, so it is, in a few hours.

LILY. He turned me out but I didn't go away. I just leant against the window-stool outside and then I walked away and then I came back and Josie was screaming. So I listened and I knew he was gone.

WILLIE. Our date is all busted up, Lily, isn't it? The very first one.

LILY. It needn't be. You could put on your coat now and come out with me.

WILLIE. No. There's too much happening to us. I'll have to stay at home to-night.

LILY (*over close to him, knotting his tie*). Are you going to knuckle under to him, Willie?

WILLIE. What do you think?

LILY. You're not.

WILLIE. You're right.

LILY. What happened to him?

WILLIE. Nothing happened to him. He was always the same. That's the mistake we made in thinking about him. He was always like that. But he was younger, and when a dictator is young his oppression doesn't fall as heavy on his subjects. We were five years free of him. When you think back on it we were never free of him before that.

LILY. Is that true or is it because he's mixed up, like you said before?

WILLIE. That man is not mixed up. He's all there. They locked him away and made him obey their rules. He'll show them. On us. No fear he won't.

LILY. What are you going to do?

WILLIE. We'll have to leave, that's all. You couldn't stay under the same roof, or he'd get on top of you again. He'd smile and beat and shout and charm until he had you in the hollow of his hand. Mebbe then he'd get nice again, once he had you. It would be farewell to Lily Green then except to see her through the window-pane knitting socks in the lamplight.

LILY. So you will marry me, Willie?

WILLIE. I'll marry you.

LILY. Nobody would ever think you were going to. Do you feel no desire to kiss me at all, Willie?

WILLIE (*her face close to his own*). Not here, Lily. Let us get out into the clean air. Not here. You haven't a notion of how much I want to.

LILY. When will we be going into the clean air?

WILLIE. Maybe to-morrow?

LILY. To-morrow is a long way away.

WILLIE. Maybe to-night. I don't know. He's gone looking for my mother. I'll have to wait until I see her. I'll have to wait and see Dovetail. I can't leave to-night. It would be running away from him, instead of just leaving.

LILY. How could there be such a change, Willie, between now and a few hours ago when we were all waiting for him to come home? Everyone had lamps lit in their breasts for him. Every sinner in the street.

WILLIE. And then he blew them out. He was always like that if you think of it. He didn't want anyone to have a lamp unless he lit it himself. If Paddo laughs everyone else must laugh. If Paddo cries we must all cry. That was always Paddo. He wanted us weepin', and when we weren't he'll set about makin' us weep.

LILY. I'm sorry for him. He must be a lonely man.

WILLIE. Not lonely. He has his own company.

LILY. That's a nice suit, Willie. Are you going to be married in that?

WILLIE. I am, and probably I'll be buried in it too. We're goin' to be shockin' poor, Lily. Did you know that?

LILY. Are we?

WILLIE. We are. Even if I cobble until the small hours of the mornin'.

LILY. We'll worry about that when we come to it. Do you think I ought to go after Josie?

WILLIE. Maybe you could talk to her.

LILY. I will.

DOVETAIL (*banging on the front door*). Come out, Paddo Reilly, come out 'll I tangle with yeh.

WILLIE. Dovetail is back with his tail up.

*He goes to the door, opens it.*

DOVETAIL. Now listen, man. . . . Oh (*squeezing his eyes*) it's you. Where's your oul' fella? (*He comes in. If he was a less hardened drinker he would be staggering, but long practice has given him command of his limbs.*) Where is he? Bring him out to me. He 'sulted me. I know well he did. God Save the King said he did and so did Munge and Panther: 'sulted me up to his face, my face, Panther's face. Where is he?

WILLIE. He's out. Sit down, Dovetail.

DOVETAIL. Mustn't sit down. Have to fight on the

feet. Have to talk up to his face. Bring him out to me.

LILY. Hello, Dovetail.

DOVETAIL *peers at her, then raises his hat carefully and bows.*

DOVETAIL. Lily, you're a lady. If I said anythin' that 'sults you, or say anythin' in the next few minutes that 'sults you, 'scuse me.

LILY. I will, Dovetail. What's bitin' you?

DOVETAIL (*approaching her*). That man. He was like a wife to me. He was also like a wife to Panther and God Save the King and Munge. They loved him deeply. I loved him deeply. We all loved him deeply, and what did he do? Tell me that.

LILY. He wouldn't marry ye.

DOVETAIL. The best years of our life he took. We med it up. Since the day we heard he was comin' back we spent five pounds eleven shillin's and ninepence at meetings of the committee to welcome him home.

WILLIE. Where did ye hold the meetings, Dovetail?

DOVETAIL. In the snug of Barney's pub. He gev it to us rent free.

WILLIE. Did ye spend the money on liquid refreshment or on bunting for the homecoming?

DOVETAIL. It went, on thinkin'. Thinkin' takes a lot a sweat outa yeh. Listen, didn't we go out last Tuesday night to Barna and load up the van with wood for the bonefire? We did that. At midnight. All for our friend Paddo, to build a bonefire. And where's the bonefire? Out, black out on the street. Never lit, it wasn't, and all the neighbours goin' out whippin' sticks offa it for the fire. Lily, I'm sad, and mad.

LILY. That's bad, Dovetail.

DOVETAIL. Have I ever hurt any man, Lily?

LILY. I wouldn't think so, Dovetail. You punish yourself at a hell of a rate, but that's all.

DOVETAIL. Why did he 'sult me, so? Wasn't I doin' it for the best? Did he welcome the kids singin' the song or did he put the run on them? He ran them. Where's me bonefire? It's black out. He quenched it. He shouldn't do that. He doesn't like me in his house. Is that the mind of a long-lost friend?

WILLIE. Dovetail, mebbe you ought to go to bed.

DOVETAIL. Are you mad, Willie? What would I be doin' in bed in the middle a the day? I gotta find Paddo. I gotta tell him he 'sulted me. Wasn't I proud to be here, Willie? You know that. Whin they'd ask me, Where you dossin' now, Dovetail, what would I say? I'd say, I'm livin' in the home oo a hero, that's what I'd say. Hero! You know somethin', Willie. Paddo is oney a paraffin-oil hero. He's oney second-grade mixture. That's why I have to see him. That's what God Save the King and Munge and Panther says: You got to say it to his face, Dovetail, they says. Paddo, you're oney a paraffin-oil hero.

WILLIE. Dovetail, you like me, don't you?

DOVETAIL. Love you, Willie. Love you deeply, and so does God Save the King and . . .

WILLIE. All right, we'll take the boys for granted. Look, Dovetail, don't talk to Paddo to-night. Leave it until the morning.

DOVETAIL (*shaking his head*). Got to talk to him to-night, Willie. Don't let night pass over your head, they say to me.

WILLIE. Dovetail, are you sure these boys are good friends of yours?

DOVETAIL. Certainly. Wouldn't they drink the last tanner I have?

LILY. They are true friends so.

WILLIE. Well, do this one favour for me, Dovetail. Don't talk to Paddo until the morning. You can say what you like to him in the morning. I'm worried, Dovetail. Honest I am. I have a lot on me mind. I don't want you on it as well. Just hold off until the morning, Dovetail.

LILY. It's only postponing it, Dovetail. It isn't as if you were dropping it altogether.

DOVETAIL. The morning?

WILLIE. Yes, sure it's nearly morning now.

DOVETAIL. 'Sright. In the morning (*Going towards the door.*) Must go back and tell God Save the King and Panther and Munge, can't call him a paraffin-oil hero until the morning. Right, Willie, 'scuse me, Lily.

*He goes out.*

WILLIE. As if we hadn't enough trouble. They can have it out in the morning if Dovetail remembers. They'll have it out anyhow. What the hell did he have to come back for? We were doing all right. We were all doing all right. And look at us now and the way he has us.

LILY. Do you want me to go now, Willie?

WILLIE. Do go, Lily. I wish you hadn't got mixed up in this. This was nothing to do with you. It makes a stain on us.

LILY. Nothing is easy, Willie. Early this evening was too easy. There would be no happy times to remember if bad times after didn't make you remember them. (*She goes to the door.*) I'll see you soon, maybe.

WILLIE. You will see me soon.

LILY. What are you going to do now?

WILLIE. What am I going to do now? I'm going to finish Finnegan's shoes, bad luck to him.

*He sits down at the bench.*

LILY. Be careful of the blue suit, Willie. You have to be married in it.

*She goes. When the door closes after her,* WILLIE *lets his head drop in his hands for a moment, then takes up his work again and bangs nails viciously into the leather. He looks up as his mother comes in the back door. She is walking carefully so as not to make any noise. She puts her shawl on the banisters and comes over.*

DAYLIA. Is he still asleep, Willie? I kem back as soon as I could.

WILLIE. No, he's not asleep. He went out looking for you.

DAYLIA (*sitting weakly on a chair*). Oh no.

WILLIE. Oh yes, you knew you shouldn't have gone. It gev him ammunition. He knocked hell out of Josie too before he went looking for you.

DAYLIA. Don't say, Willie. What's got into him?

WILLIE. It isn't what's got into him, but what never left him.

DAYLIA. Why was he lookin' for me, Willie?

WILLIE. He wanted to stop you drinking.

DAYLIA. But I wasn't drinking, Willie. I tould you I wasn't drinkin'. You should have tould him I wasn't drinkin'. Didn't I only go out to get a little message with Bid? And where did I go then? I went into the chapel to pray, Willie. I declare to God I did.

WILLIE. I thought you might.

DAYLIA. Prayin' to God, I was, to make us happy. Because we were happy for a long time now, despite your father wasn't with us, and I had to pray that he would be happy with us. Did he hurt Josie, Willie?

WILLIE. He must have. He hurted her worse inside than outside. She said she will never come home again.

DAYLIA. Oh no, Willie. Oh no.

WILLIE. Oh yes, Mother, oh yes. There's no use blinking it any more. He's back now and he's worse than ever he was, and he'll make the life of the lot of us pure hell unless we get away from him.

DAYLIA (*rising and coming over to him*). You mustn't do that, Willie. Willie, you mustn't do that. Make a promise to me, Willie. You won't go away.

WILLIE. I can't promise that, Mother. I'm going to marry Lily Green. So I have to go away.

DAYLIA. You're going to marry Lily Green! Why wasn't I tould, Willie? Why didn't you tell me? I'm your mother, Willie, and I never know nothin' until it's all over.

WILLIE. I couldn't tell you something that was oney fixed up this evenin'.

DAYLIA. Oh, but I'm glad, Willie. I'm rale glad. It warms me inside, so it does. She's a nice girl, so she is. You deserve something nice, Willie, the way you looked after us while your father was away. But that's good, Willie. When Dovetail and Bid get a nice place of their own and move on, can't you move into the big room upstairs? It would be grand for ye, Willie. Wouldn't it be the very thing?

WILLIE. No.

DAYLIA. But why, Willie? Wouldn't we be all together then?

WILLIE. That's it, Mother. That's the reason. The time has come for me to leave the nest. To fly away, to carve out a life of me own. Because that's the only way we could have any chance in the pursuit, and Paddo doesn't want me to marry Lily Green. Paddo is goin' to do everythin' in his power to stop me from marryin' Lily Green.

DAYLIA. What has he agin it?

WILLIE. He doesn't think I should marry the daughter of the man he killed. Apart from that he has nothing agin it except he doesn't like to see anybody happy.

DAYLIA. Maybe there's something in it, Willie. Maybe you ought to listen to your father.

WILLIE. That was a quick change, Mother. You back him up to the hilt, don't you? Well, he can go to hell.

DAYLIA. Willie, you can't leave me alone here with him.

WILLIE. Why?

DAYLIA. God help me, I'm afraid of him, Willie. I'm afraid of him. Don't leave me alone with him. For the love and honour of God, don't leave me alone with him.

WILLIE. Look, Mother, don't pull that one on me. I have my own life to lead. You have nothing to be afraid of. He knows he has you. He can do what he likes with you. You have no need to be afraid of him.

DAYLIA. I can't ever say it, Willie. I never never said it. Just the three of us here. It was a good life, Willie. I wasn't afraid nor nothin'. Those years. They were like a smart dream, Willie. Now unless God changes him, it will be the same as it always was, and I'll lie awake in

88

the darkness thinkin' of what the mornin' will bring.
Don't leave me, Willie, if you have any love at all for me.

WILLIE. Mother, what are you trying to do to me?

DAYLIA. Honest to God I'm not tryin' to do anythin'
to you, Willie. You are young and Lily is young.
Haven't ye yeer whole life ahead of ye? Ye don't have
to do things in a hurry. Don't leave me, Willie, for a
while, for a short while until he has settled down and
become himself. Just to hold on for a while, Willie,
until he is workin' agin and things will be the same as
before.

WILLIE. You know what'll happen. He'll get around
you. He'll get around me. He'll work hard on that
until he gets what he's afther. Then he'll have the lot of
us tied into knots again with nothing in the future to free
us until death takes a hold of him. No, Mother, I can't
do it, I tell you. If I don't free meself now I will be
finished.

BID (*coming in the back door*). Is it there you are, Daylia,
and I lookin' all over for you? What happened you?
Wasn't meself and Paddo crisscrossin' one another in
every pub in the town lookin' for you, and isn't it a pity
he's an abstainer? The white face of you I told him
would be the betther for a touch of Guinness's bloom.

DAYLIA. Into the chapel I went.

BID. God bless us, it's a saint you are. Wasn't I
standin' up talkin' to pass the time with the poor Cassidy
woman, God help her, and she crucified with crosses, and
when I look around not a sight or sound of you to be
seen! Tell me, himself is not himself yet. He has a
strained look of constirpation on him and I must say he
was a bit short with me, he was indeed. What would

have happened your family, I was goin' to tell him, if meself and Dovetail hadn't chipped in ten bob a week for the room all the time you was away on your holidays?

DAYLIA. It wasn't that great help at all, Bid. Didn't we let ye in from the charity of our hearts and ye not havin' a roof over yeer heads except the tin of the van and that leakin'?

BID. Now, Daylia O'Reilly, my readin' of the thing is different entirely. I says to Dovetail, they are there without two happence to bless themselves with, with the poor Willie hammerin' oul' leather from mornin' to night and the little girl sellin' drawers for five shillin's a week in your man's dashery. We'll take their room, I says, and be a great help to them. Do we get any thanks now at all for it in the heel of the hunt? We do not. Abuse and things and Paddo lookin' at us as if we had the foot-and-mouth disease.

DAYLIA (*expending some of her worry*). You mustn't talk like that. Is it everybody in the street that would have taken ye in? Ye couldn't get a burrow in the place if it wasn't for the kindness of our hearts, with Dovetail dumpin' dirty things in the yard like skinned rabbits and oul' sheep's wool, and the time he brought in the live goat and smelled us up so that we didn't get rid of it for three months. What kind of people but saints would have put up with things like that?

BID. True enough. I see! Now, madam. We see the people now in their true colours, so we do. Indeed we do. Furnished room you were to give us. What kind of furniture — back-breakin' bed with a mattress as thin as a sheet of paper, with wires stickin' into your guts, and cracked teapots that wouldn't hould a teaspoon a water!

Oh, indeed ! And an oul' mirror on the table that was riddled with wood maggots and cracked and bent so that every time you looked into it you thought you were lookin' at a monster.

DAYLIA. The mirror doesn't lie, ma'am.

BID. Bedammed to you, ma'am, and your furnished room. A danger to life and limb every bit of the bloody furniture, havin' to come down the stairs at night and risk pneumonia runnin' out to the closet because the commodity was a rusty bit a machinery peppered like a granulator. Furnished rooms at ten bob a week that you wouldn't put the cat inta.

DAYLIA. You say now what you think. Why didn't you say what you think all the times you had the chance ? That's the brave woman for you.

WILLIE. For God's sake will ye shut up ? Ye've been at this once a month. Ye have these rows flogged to death. Be quiet, can't ye ? Now is no time for them.

BID. Kept me mouth shut because I was a lady. That's why. Because I was well brought up, that's why, with me lovely mother washin' floors above in the convent.

DAYLIA. Far away from convents you were dragged up, ma'am. They left small impression on your black soul, ma'am, that would turn like that and bite the hand that rescued ye from the streets of the town.

BID. May God in Heaven look down and forgive you for the desecration !

WILLIE. Sweet hour !

DAYLIA. No time there wasn't that ye couldn't have taken up yeer few miserable possessions and gone about yeer business, plaguing someone else like the flyin' grasshoppers. Any time at all, ma'am.

BID. God give me patience with you! How many times did I want to leave yeer kip but me lovely Dovetail wouldn't let me? We can't do it, Bid, he says. We'd have it on our souls until eternity that we left them starvin' in their mean little house.

DAYLIA. Well, now, there's no need for ye. There's no need for ye.

PADDO (*coming in. He has been at the back door for the past few speeches*). No need, indeed. No need for drunken quarrels on me first night at home. A grand welcome for a man on his first night at home to have his wife in the middle of a porter quarrel with the upstairs lodger!

DAYLIA. No, no, Paddo, we weren't quarrellin'. We were oney exchangin' a few remarks.

PADDO. For you, ma'am (*to* BID), ye can have until twelve a'clock to-morra to gather all yeer bits and pieces and get out of here. Get to hell out of here or I'll gup and get them out of here for ye.

DAYLIA. No, no, Paddo, Bid didn't mean what she was sayin'. We were just worried, that's all. We didn't mane what we said at all, the pair of us.

BID. Sure you wouldn't take the few words serious, Paddo. Man, if a person didn't have the few words to blow off steam once in a while they'd bust like an engine.

PADDO. I don't care what they'd bust like, ma'am. I don't care what kind of a few words ye were havin'. Ye should never have been let into this place. It would have been betther to starve than to let the likes of ye move in above. That's all. Now I'm tellin' ye, ye have until to-morra at twelve to get out of it.

BID. You can't do that to us, Mister O'Reilly. It's

not easy to find a place to move to that quick. What harm have we done you?

PADDO. You've done me a lot of harm. Have a look at the face of me wife and see what harm ye've done me.

DAYLIA. Paddo, don't be hasty. Moves can't be made as quick as that. Give them a bit of time.

PADDO. I'm givin' them time. I'm givin' them until to-morra, amn't I? They are more than lucky that I don't put the run on them to-night.

DAYLIA. A person can't find a room that quick, Paddo.

PADDO. Shut up. Stop talkin' back. If you are that tender-hearted about them you should have been out lookin' for a place for them instead of sneakin' around all the pubs in the town.

DAYLIA. I wasn't, Paddo. I wasn't, on me oath I wasn't. Wasn't I down in the chapel sayin' a few prayers? Bid knows I was.

PADDO. Get into the room.

DAYLIA. On me oath, Paddo, I was down in the chapel.

PADDO. Get into the room when I tell you!

DAYLIA (*after a pause*). All right, Paddo, I'll do what you say. I'll get into the room.

*She goes into the room slowly. They watch her.*

PADDO. I have no more to say to you now, ma'am. You know my mind.

*He turns away from her. She goes to mount the stairs.*

BID. I do now, Mister O'Reilly. I thought I did before but I wasn't right about you. I know what you are now, right enough. We'll start lookin' for a place in the mornin'. We'll get on all right, Mister O'Reilly. But I don't know what's goin' to happen to you.

*She goes.* PADDO *stands a moment looking at* WILLIE

*who is working away. Then he follows* DAYLIA *into
the room. The door closes decisively.* WILLIE *keeps
hammering for a time but then the hammering slowly
dies away as he listens. There is no sound from the
room. The silence is more sinister than screams. He
taps away again indecisively. Finally he leaves down
the hammer, takes up his knife, looks at it, gets up
slowly and walks over to the room door. He calls.*

WILLIE. Mother, Mother, come out here and make me
a sup of tea. Do you hear? I want a cup of tea. I'm
parched with the thirst. If you want the money out of
Finnegan, better come out and make me a sup of tea.
(*He listens. There is no answer. He bangs on the door.*)
Mother, are you comin' out to make the sup of tea or do
I have to go in for you?

*This elicits a reply. He has spoken very determinedly.
The door opens. His mother comes out. He looks at
her closely. She is avoiding his eyes. She looks pale
and hopeless. She goes over towards the fire.*

DAYLIA. I'll make you a sup of tay, Willie. (*She takes
up the teapot.*) I'll g'out and empty the tea-leaves.

*He stops her as she goes to pass.*

WILLIE. Mother, what did he do to you? Tell me,
what did he do to you?

DAYLIA. Nothin', Willie, nothin' at all. Honest to
God, nothin' at all. (*She passes him by quickly. He looks
after her, then looks at the closed door of the room, his teeth
clenched. Then he goes back to the bench, throws down the knife,
grabs the hammer and expends his dumb anger on the leather.
She comes back with the teapot. She stirs up the fire under the
kettle. Then she sits on the stool below the fire with her back
half-turned to him.*) It won't be long now, Willie. The

94

kettle'll soon be boiled. (*There is another long silence, then she speaks again.*) Willie.

WILLIE. Yes, Mother?

DAYLIA. You and Lily Green get married, Willie, and go away. You'll do that, Willie, won't you? Promise me, Willie.

WILLIE. And leave you here on your own with him?

DAYLIA. That doesn't matther, Willie. Honest, that doesn't matter. You go and be happy, Willie. Promise me that.

WILLIE. I won't promise you that now, Mother, no more than I would promise you the reverse of it a while back. We'll wait and see.

> *There is a heavy knock on the front door.* WILLIE *gets up and goes to it. He opens it.* MANCHESTER *comes in. He has his two hands buried in his coat pockets.*

MANCHESTER. Hello, Willie.

WILLIE. Hello, Manchester.

MANCHESTER. Hello, ma'am. How are you? I haven't met you before.

DAYLIA. How do you do, Mister Monaghan?

MANCHESTER. Where is he? Bring him out to me.

WILLIE. Who? Paddo, is it?

MANCHESTER. That's right. The one and only Paddo. Trot him out.

WILLIE. You're sure you know what you're doin', Manchester?

MANCHESTER. I know what I'm doing, Willie. Let me have him.

WILLIE. If you are sure you know what you are doing, Manchester, I will be delighted to let you have him.

> *Pleased, he goes towards the room.*

DAYLIA. No trouble, Mister Monaghan. For God's sake no trouble. We have enough trouble on us now.

MANCHESTER. This is no trouble at all, ma'am. It's pure pleasure.

WILLIE. Paddo, there's a visitor here wants to see you. (*He comes back, sits at the bench.*) You'll excuse me, Manchester, if I go on working?

MANCHESTER. You earn the old salt, Willie.

PADDO. Who is it?

*He sees who it is.*

MANCHESTER. That's right, Paddo, it's me.

PADDO. I told you what'd happen you if you put a foot in this house.

MANCHESTER. That's right, Paddo, you told me what'd happen.

PADDO (*moving towards him*). Now there's no need to tell you a second time.

MANCHESTER. Halt there now, Paddo. (*He takes his two hands out of his pockets. They are decorated with chromium-plated knuckle-dusters.*) You had me fazed there a while back. I didn't know how to treat you. I was sorry for you. You were the oul' fella of the girl I wanted to marry. Now I know what you are, Paddo. You're just a goddam bully, that's all you are. A strong man who is not afraid to use his great strength on people not as strong as himself, like old Pat Green, or like taking a buckle to your daughter.

PADDO. Get out of here.

MANCHESTER. Now, Paddo, I'm going to wallop you. I've never been in jail in me life, Paddo, but I'm willin' to go to jail for you. Just for this once. Every day of it will be a pleasure.

DAYLIA. Mister Monaghan, Mister Monaghan, please go away.

MANCHESTER. You go somewhere else, ma'am. This isn't going to be nice. You can stay if you like and watch. I don't care. Your daughter Josie was with me, ma'am. He has her back torn in pieces. You didn't know that maybe. And she wants me to go somewhere and sleep with her. Did you ever hear the like of that, a grand decent girl that I'm goin' to marry? Yes, I knew then there was only one thing to do with your man. To give him something that he's never had all his life. To let him be on the gettin' end for the first time in a bloody misspent life. You have me mad, Paddo. You have me so mad that nothing under the sun will cure me except the lettin' of your blood. I'm goin' to pound you, Paddo, make no mistake about it. I'm goin' to pound you into pulp.

PADDO. Willie, go on down and get the Guards for him.

WILLIE. I haven't time, Paddo, I'm mendin' shoes.

PADDO. Now get out of here, Monaghan. (*He puts his hands on the back of a chair and raises it off the ground.*) I don't want to be responsible for your life, do you hear?

MANCHESTER. You can be, Paddo. You can have my life if you want it, but you'll be only a tattered remnant be the time you have it in your hand. I'm comin' for you now, Paddo, and may the guardian angel of loud-mouthed boastin' bastards protect you.

DAYLIA. No, no, Mister Monaghan, don't do it!

MANCHESTER *moves towards him.* PADDO *raises the chair in his hands.* MANCHESTER *swerves, dodges, moves in, grabs the rungs of the chair with one hand and*

97

*raises the other knuckle-dustered hand to bring it down.
There is nothing to stop it crunching into* PADDO'S
*face except* JOSIE'S *voice from the door. It is loud
and penetrating.*

JOSIE. No, no, stop it, Manchester! Manchester, do
you hear me!

*She has grabbed his falling arm. The blaze goes out of*
MANCHESTER'S *eyes, the fear out of* PADDO'S.
MANCHESTER *falls back.*

MANCHESTER. You shouldn't have stopped me, Josie.
You should have waited until I got a few cracks at him.

JOSIE. What'll that solve? Wasn't it blows that made
us what we are? What's the use of makin' more of it?

MANCHESTER. If you say so. But he won't get another
chance to have a bash at you. Get your few things
together now and move out of here. I'll fix up a good
digs for you until later on.

JOSIE. No, Manchester, I'm not moving out.

MANCHESTER. Are you mad?

JOSIE. No. He has us by the hasp, you see. How can
we move out and think of Mother left with him?

MANCHESTER. Bring your mother too. Let the whole
lot of ye move out on him. Leave him his house that
nobody will be allowed to put a foot in.

JOSIE. You wouldn't go, Mother, would you?

PADDO. She has a sense of decency which none of you
have. Thank God there is one person in the house that
I can fall back on.

DAYLIA. Are you mad, Josie? What would I be
walkin' away from your father for? I think yeer all
queer. The queer evenin' has got into ye. Everything
will be all right in the mornin'.

JOSIE. Everything will not be all right in the mornin'. That's what you said time and time before when he was cruel to you. You know you said it before.

PADDO. Make up your mind now, girl. Go with that man if you are going and stay if you are stayin'. If he waits here much longer I won't be responsible for me actions.

JOSIE. Go, Manchester, and leave us. There's nothin' left to us but a bit of foolish pride, that we want to hide it from the neighbours what a sad case we are in.

MANCHESTER. Well, will I see you agin?

JOSIE. You will, Manchester. You will see me agin.

MANCHESTER. And listen, if he lays one finger-nail on you, somethin' serious will happen to him. Does he know that?

JOSIE. He probably knows that now, Manchester.

MANCHESTER. Right. Good night, Josie (*He crosses over to her and kisses her.*) That's the first and it won't be the last, but it's an honest one. I was serious when he put the run on me first. You know that now, don't you?

JOSIE. I do, Manchester.

MANCHESTER. I'd do time for you, Josie.

JOSIE. What I want you to do is not to do time for me, Manchester.

MANCHESTER. Well, I can do that too.

JOSIE. Diggin' spuds in the spring?

MANCHESTER. Anythin' you like, Josie. (*He goes to the door, turns there.*) And I meant it about that pram too with the cream lace affair on it, and I won't whip it. On me oath I won't. I know somewhere we can get it it whole-sale.

*He winks broadly at her and goes.*

99

PADDO (*to* WILLIE). He was goin' to attack me and you wouldn't raise a finger. You wouldn't do a thing and he was goin' after me with weapons. What kind of blood have you in you at all?

WILLIE. Your blood, Paddo. Didn't you know?

JOSIE. I'm goin' up to me room, Mother. If you want me you know where to find me.

DAYLIA. Can't you wait and have a sup a tay, Josie? Can't we all sit down and be peaceable and have a sup a tay?

JOSIE. Thanks, Mother, I don't want it. (*She goes to the stairs.*) I met Lily, Willie. She was talkin' to me. She says she'll be waiting for you when you are ready to go out.

*They watch her go up the stairs.*

PADDO. You see how right I was? Isn't it a strange thing what a few strokes of the strap will do? That's what I tell you, Willie. You should have got after her. In a few weeks' time this house will be back to normal. All this past will be behind us and we will be happy.

WILLIE. Is the tea ready, Mother? I have a terrible thirst.

DAYLIA (*as he comes over to the table*). I'll pour it now, amac.

PADDO. None of ye have any idea about the ideas of liberty until someone takes it away from ye. I know. I know what it was to be bound up, with never a minute that belonged to yourself. Even in your sleep your mind couldn't go free. These things. This is what should happen to ye for a while so that ye'd learn how to conduct yeerselves.

WILLIE. You're not talking about liberty, Paddo.

You're talkin' about licence. You didn't learn much. All you learned was because somebody took away your liberty, you'd take away ours. Well, you had it coming to you. We have done nothing except try to live.

*He turns his head as* DOVETAIL *comes in the door.* DOVETAIL *stands there in the door, looking at them. He opens his mouth to say something, catches* WILLIE'S *eye and closes it again. He reaches up with his hands, has a little difficulty in finding his lips, but when he does find them he stitches them together with his fingers, then holding on to them he moves towards the stairs. He has one foot on the bottom step when* PADDO *speaks.*

PADDO. Here, you, don't go up for a minute, I have something to say to you. (DOVETAIL *looks at him, makes an effort and then shakes his head and goes on.*) Come back till I talk to you, do you hear me? What the hell is up with you, man, apart from being drunk?

DOVETAIL (*taking his hands away*). There's nothin' up with me, you . . . (*He sees* WILLIE *looking at him.*) Sorry, Willie, very sorry.

*He continues up the stairs.*

PADDO. Listen, do you want to madden me? Stay where you are until I talk to you. (DOVETAIL *stands still on the stairs with his back to him.*) I was already talkin' to your woman. I don't know whether she understood me.

DOVETAIL (*turning on him*). You leave her alone. Great man. Great man talkin' to women. No man talkin' to men.

PADDO. Yeer to get out of here be midday to-morra, bag and baggage, or I put ye mesel, do you hear?

DOVETAIL. I hear, hero. Hero me eye. Know what

you are ?  You're a paraffin-oil hero, that's what you are,
Misther Paddo O'Reilly.

WILLIE.  Dovetail !

DOVETAIL.  Sorry, Willie, very sorry.  Couldn't hould
it in.  Med an effort like a man, but the hero drug it outa
me.  You know what they think about you now, Paddo ?
Stinking, you are, in the noses of the citizens.  No good,
Paddo.  No bloody good.

PADDO.  Do you think I care for the opinions of a pack
of drunken rowdies ?

DOVETAIL.  Should care, Paddo.  Know a man be his
friends.  Have you any friends now, Paddo ?  No friends.
Wouldn't throw you a rope in a swalla hole.  Not a
friend.

PADDO.  You be out of here.  I told you.

DOVETAIL.  Not goin', Paddo.  Not gettin' rid of me
that easy.  You wait and see.  May be a small man in
stature, but I'm a tiger when I'm vexed.  Tangle with
me, man, and I'll sharpen me eye teeth in yeh.  Not
movin'.  Main force and ignorance oney weapons.  Kept
a roof over the heads of your family when you were away
on the holidays.  Not goin' now till I'm good and ready.
Have min at me back to defind me.  Have to bate me,
Paddo, and bate me friends of the rearguard, God Save
the King and Panther and Munge.  You prick me, man,
and they bleed.

PADDO.  Shut up now.  You say much more and you'll
go out on top of your head this minute.

DOVETAIL.  You're a small man.  A small piddlin' little
man.  That's what you are.  Y'aren't worth a dried spit
in the dust.  I'll go whin I'm good and ready and not a
minute before.  Hold on to that now, hero.

*He goes on up.*

PADDO. You've said enough now. Out with you. You hear. Out with you now this very minute. Come back when I tell you. By God, if you won't I'll haul you back by the hair of the skull.

*He moves up the stairs after him.*

WILLIE (*rising*). Leave him alone, Paddo. He's drunk. He doesn't know what he's saying.

DAYLIA. Paddo! Paddo!

PADDO (*out of sight*). Come on now. Out into the street with you where you belong, you drunken trickey.

DOVETAIL (*out of sight. His voice raised in a shout*). Hands off, you Mullingar murderer. Hands off your betthers, Judas O'Reilly.

WILLIE (*who has one of* FINNEGAN'S *shoes in his hands*). If you hit him I'll go for you, Paddo. On me oath if you hit him I'll go for you!

PADDO. Out with you, you dirty little bum.

DOVETAIL. Here's a blow for Ireland. Up the poor oul' Republic!

WILLIE. Don't hit him, Paddo! I told you not to hit him. I told you! I told you! (*He fires the shoe up the stairs with all his strength. There is a confused noise from the landing, and* DOVETAIL *comes tumbling down the stairs. He stays where he has fallen at* WILLIE'S *feet.*) You did it! You did it! Every instinct in you is cryin' out to hit somebody. All the time hit somebody. Strike around you like a maniac until the whole world is down in the dirt at your feet.

PADDO (*coming down the stairs*). You hit me. You hit me with the shoe. (*He has his hand up to the side of his head. He takes it away. There is blood on his palm.*) I'm bleedin'.

You have me bleedin'. What kind of nature is in you to strike your own father ?

WILLIE. Oh, God, is there no way of gettin' through you ? Is there no way at all of you openin' your eyes and seein' what you are ? Hey, Dovetail, get up. Get up, do you hear me ? (DOVETAIL *doesn't move. He is lying on his face.* WILLIE *gets down on his knee. He shakes him.*) Dovetail ! (DOVETAIL *doesn't move at all.* WILLIE'S *voice becomes anxious. He turns him over on his back. He is lying supine.*) Dovetail ! (*He looks up slowly at his father.*) You've done it again, Paddo. You have done it again. You've killed your second man.

DAYLIA. Oh no !

PADDO (*anxiously*). He's not kilt, I tell you. He's only puttin' it on. (*He comes down the stairs, kneels down at the other side of* DOVETAIL.) Here, get up, do you hear me ? Get up. Goddam you, get up out of that, when I tell you !

> DOVETAIL *doesn't move.* PADDO *rises and stands up rubbing his palms down the sides of his trousers.*

WILLIE. That's it, Paddo. I told you not to hit him. What are you going to do now, Paddo ? How many years will they put you away for this time ? Will it be double or treble, will it ?

DAYLIA. Oh, no. He's not hurtit. (*She goes over, shakes* DOVETAIL.) Dovetail, get up like a good man and don't have the life worried out of us. (*He doesn't move. She gets up again, backs away.*) Oh my God, what are we going to do ?

WILLIE. We'll do what we always done before. We'll call the Guards and tell them it was oney an accident like it was before. That he couldn't help it. That he wasn't drunk like he was when he killed his first man, only that he lost his temper.

DAYLIA. Willie, stop it, can't you ? Can't you stop it ?

PADDO. I couldn't face it again. I couldn't face this again. I didn't mean to hit him. I only gave him a tap, I tell ye. He was drunk. He fell down the stairs. He must ha' fallen on his head. That's what happened. It wasn't my fault.

WILLIE. That's a good story now. Stick to that story now and they mightn't hang you until the next time.

DAYLIA. Willie, Willie, don't be torturin' him.

WILLIE. I'm not torturin' him. I'm only tellin' him the truth. I knew something like this would happen again. If it didn't happen to-day it would happen to-morra or the day afther. Always, always. Why didn't somebody make him suffer before ? All the things he has done that never saw the light when you should have been out screamin' in the streets what he was doin' to us. It's too late now. Too late.

PADDO. I won't go through it again. I swear that. I couldn't face it again. Not another time. I didn't mean it.

WILLIE. They won't believe you.

PADDO. Then they'll have to find me. I'm going to go. It was all for the best. God above in heaven knows that I am right. I was right to bring ye back to what ye were created for. I was right to put that thing out of the house and the way she was underminin' Daylia. It had to be done. But nobody will ever believe. Ever believe. Nobody ever believes the truth of things.

BID *comes down the stairs screaming.*

BID. Oh, Dovetail, Dovetail, me lovely Dovetail, what

has the murderer done to you? (*She gets on her knees behind him and lifts his head on to her lap.*) Speak to me, Dovetail. Open your lovely lips and address your Bridget. He's dead. He's kilt. He's a corpse. Oh, Dovetail! Dovetail! (*She looks up at* PADDO.) You dirty murderer! I knew you'd do it. We all knew you'd do it. Not one a the neighbours could rest in their beds afraid a y' comin' in through the winda. You killed me lovely husband, but you won't get away with it. I'm not Mrs. Green, you scoundrel, forgivin' and forgettin'. Speak to me, Dovetail. For the love of God speak to me!

PADDO. You don't understand. He fell, I tell yeh. I didn't hit him. I oney had a hould of him and when Willie flung a shoe at me I let him go and he must ha' fallen on his head. I didn't hit him, ma'am. I swear I didn't hit him.

BID *doesn't answer him. She rushes to the door. She flings it open. She shouts into the street. The light is dying in the sky.*

BID. Wake up, let ye! He's done it again. Paddo has kilt again. He's knocked the light out of me lovely Dovetail. Send for the Guards. Paddo Reilly did it agin. (*She turns back.*) The day they hang you I want to be there, you monster. I'll put the rope around your neck with me own hands. (*She goes back to* DOVETAIL, *cradles his head in her lap, sways with him as she speaks. You can't escape the suspicion that she is enjoying herself.*) I loved you, Dovetail, from your double crown to the tips of your shoes. You were the best man in Ireland, me darling, until he crippled yeh. What will poor oul' Bid do now, without her husband? Who will hold her hand now in the spring evenings lookin' at the daffodils in the woods and the birds cryin' in the strange places ? Oh, speak to me, Dovetail. Speak to your lonely widow.

DOVETAIL. O-o-o-o-oh, what hit me ?

    BID *is so startled, she screams and starts back from him and lets his head fall on the floor.* DOVETAIL *groans again.*

DAYLIA. He's not dead.

WILLIE. How could he be dead ? It'd take more than that to kill Dovetail.

PADDO (*coming over to him*). You knew there was nothing wrong with him. You knew all the time there was nothing wrong with him.

WILLIE. Yes, Paddo. It's only your guilty conscience that sees corpses all around you.

PADDO. Why did you do it ? Tell me, Willie, why did you do a cruel thing like that to me ? I thought he was dead. I could have swore an oath he was dead. Did you stop and think what you med me suffer there for a long time ?

WILLIE. Won't it do you good, Paddo ? Won't it startle you to think how easy it is for you to kill a man again ? Dovetail isn't dead but he could be, Paddo. He could be a corpse again and you could be facing the same thing all over again, and we could be facing it all over again. Just one blow, Paddo, like before, and you have us all suffering again with you.

PADDO. You're unnatural, Willie. You have no love or liking in you at all.

WILLIE. What cause have I ever had for love or liking, Paddo ? What cause have you ever given us ?

PADDO. I see.

BID. Dovetail, Dovetail, are you really all right? You're not dead, Dovetail?

DOVETAIL (*sitting up*). I wish I was dead. I have an awful head on me. The curse a hell on that fella below and his bad whiskey. What am I doin' here on the floor?

BID. Paddo kilt you and you fell down the stairs and we near had you in a coffin.

DOVETAIL. Oh yes, Paddo. I remember, Paddo. Paddo was tellin' me to buzz outa here at twelve o'clock to-morra. You hear that, Bid? Well, we'll go, so we will, and we'll go with dignity. Help me up. (*She does so.*)

PADDO. You can stay or go, whatever you like, man. I was puttin' the wrong person out of here. There's only one person in this house that's not wanted in it and that's Paddo Reilly.

DAYLIA. Please, Paddo, stop talkin' like that.

PADDO. That's right. Is it the first time in history that a man is chased away from his home by his own children?

WILLIE. Stop it now, Paddo, nobody is chasin' you away. Don't saddle us again with your own resolutions.

PADDO. What else can I do? Haven't ye defeated me? Won't ye make me name smell in the town with yeer tales if I stay with ye? Once the thought struck me when I was walking the long road to the station. Will I walk past it now, I said, into the freedom of the green fields? And I thought of ye waitin' at home for me around the fire with the light lit in yeer eyes and food on the table and the place shinin' and I'd walk into me home and I would be at peace after all me torture. Was that what I walked inta? Think over what I walked inta!

WILLIE. You don't have to walk out of it. I'll walk

out of it and Josie will walk out of it and you can have it for your own.

DAYLIA. For the love of God stop talkin' like that, let ye. What will the people say?

PADDO. People forget, Daylia. You can remember that. They forget more when they have nothin' to look at. Remember that. I'll see you again some time. Maybe later when we are a bit older and our children have given up rulin' our lives for us. Remember that. That I said that. I will send you things. I will go now the way I came. Out the back door I will go sneakin' like an animal. When me wounds are healed I will come back to you.

*He turns and walks out.* DAYLIA *is petrified, then she runs after him.*

DAYLIA. Paddo, Paddo, come back, will you? It's wrong, Paddo. They are all sorry. They didn't know what they were sayin', Paddo. Paddo!

*She follows him out into the yard calling his name.*

JOSIE (*from the stairs where she has been listening for some time*). Does he mean that now or will he be back again in the morning?

WILLIE. I don't know. I honestly don't know. Did he want to leave us all the time and was that what he was leading up to or what?

BID. He's an odd sort of man. He'd fricken yeh. Do we have to leave to-morra, Willie?

WILLIE. You don't have to leave to-morrow, Bid, or any other day.

BID. Thank God, I hope he doesn't ever come back. All the welcome we had for him and what happened to it!

TRAPPER (*coming in the door*). I thought you were dead, Dovetail, or is it a walkin' corpse you are?

DOVETAIL. I'm near.   Listen, has Paddo really moved out ?

TRAPPER. Is Paddo gone again ?

WILLIE. He walked out the door, turning his back on his ungrateful children.

TRAPPER. That's quare.   He wasn't cured so ?

WILLIE. Maybe he's cured now.   I don't know.

TRAPPER. Do you think he's gone for good ?

WILLIE. I don't know.   He might be at that.

TRAPPER. That's sad.

DOVETAIL. What's sad about it ?   Didn't he turn into a mortal inimy a the people ?   Wasn't he near pullin' the guts out 'f his best friend ?   Hey !

TRAPPER. What's got into you now ?

DOVETAIL. Listen, that bonefire.   How about that bonefire ?

TRAPPER. How about it ?

DOVETAIL. This.   When he wouldn't let us light it to welcome him home, why can't we light it to celebrate him goin' away ?   Hah ?

TRAPPER. Now, Dovetail, you have an idea there.   The whole of the street is at their doors waitin' to see the blood flowin' out of O'Reilly's.   It might be a good idea to give them a spectacle to take their minds off it.

DOVETAIL. A bit a paraffin oil, Willie.   For the love a God give 's a bit a paraffin oil.

WILLIE. There's a bottle in the corner there.

DOVETAIL *goes over for it.*

DOVETAIL. Come on, Bid, we'll light it.   Get a brand from the fire and we'll set the red flames dancin' in the sky for them.   (*He goes towards the door.*)   Listen, I knew it. I knew even when he quenched it that I'd get the bonefire. God would ha' died or given me that bonefire. (*He goes into the street shouting*) Hey, kids, kids, it's on agin! The bonefire is on agin! Dovetail is back from the grave!

BID (*who has taken a coal from the fire and is going out after him blowing on it, holding it with the tongs*). Thank God he's not dead on me. I don't know what I'd do if Dovetail was dead on me. He's like a lucky package, so he is. You never know what you'll pull out next. (*She goes out of the door calling*) Hey, Dovetail, me darling, wait for me.

> *It is rather dark in the kitchen.* TRAPPER *goes over and sits in a stool by the fire.* JOSIE *is still standing on the stairs and* WILLIE *is standing near his bench.*

TRAPPER. Finnegan is fumin' about those shoes, Willie.

WILLIE. Yes, Finnegan. Finnegan must have his shoes. (*He sits at the bench.*) That was where you came in before, Trapper.

TRAPPER. Yes, and what has happened since?

WILLIE. You tell him, Josie.

JOSIE (*coming down the stairs*). I don't know. We were nearly destroyed or were we? What did you think of us all, Trapper, last night, say, before he came?

TRAPPER. I thought it was a happy little house. I did that. I thought it was a rare place to come for a laugh or a chat. There was nothin' upsettin' ye, oney small things that make people happy anyhow.

JOSIE. I thought we were happy too. He was out to destroy that. Maybe we weren't happy, Willie, were we?

WILLIE. We were. He would have destroyed us.

JOSIE. What about Mother, Willie? What will Mother do without him?

WILLIE. She will cry a lot. Have you ever seen a dog that is terrified of its master? I have. It's a terrified love, sort of. That's what she has for him.

LILY (*from the door*). Hello.

TRAPPER. Hello, Lily. Come in, won't you?

LILY. It's dark in here. Why don't ye light the lamp?

WILLIE. The darkness is nice too. Like the touch of velvet.

> *In truth you can barely see their faces now in the flickering light of the fire.* LILY *comes over and stands behind* WILLIE. *She lays a hand on his shoulder.*

LILY. All the talking in the street. Is it true that Paddo killed Dovetail and hanged himself and shot Willie? I'm only asking because I saw Dovetail's ghost out there blowing into a bonefire surrounded by all the kids, and that's what everyone is saying.

WILLIE. It's a bit exaggerated.

LILY. Are you comin' out for a walk?

WILLIE. Am I comin' for a walk? Yes, I am. Why wouldn't I? What's to stop me now?

TRAPPER. Finnegan. For the love of God and humanity, finish Finnegan's shoes or he'll have his finger-nails bit down to his wrist.

WILLIE. Right-o. First we'll finish Finnegan's shoes. Then we'll walk.

JOSIE (*who is leaning against the cupboard*). It was excitin' all the same while it lasted. Did ye see the fierce look on Manchester's face?

WILLIE. He was like a tiger.

JOSIE. Sure Manchester is not too bad now, Willie, all the same?

WILLIE. Manchester is all right, Josie. He'd be a handy brother-in-law.

TRAPPER. You're a queer one really, Willie.

WILLIE. How do you mean, Trapper?

TRAPPER. You're a deep one, Willie. You look so quiet and harmless bending over a last, but you have deep things in you. You're what the fellas in the books call the engineerin' god or something. You understand me, Willie?

WILLIE. I don't know, Trapper.

TRAPPER. Leave it like that. Maybe all you engineered was for the best.

LILY. He was a poor engineer about me, now. I had to do a lot of work there by meself.

TRAPPER. That's different.

JOSIE. Wouldn't Manchester kill you? Did ye hear him talkin' about the cream lace cover on the pram?

WILLIE. Yes.

TRAPPER. Willie, would it be possible sometimes for you maybe to play a few boards of draughts with me?

WILLIE. It would, Trapper, but I don't know much about draughts.

TRAPPER. You'll learn, Willie. You'll learn very fast indeed, I'd say, and it wouldn't surprise me that you'd learn soon to wallop me.

> *They are silent as the back door opens.* DAYLIA *comes in. When you see her eyes in the firelight you see that she has been weeping. She wipes her eyes now with the hem of her apron. She sits on the bench above the fire. She speaks.*

DAYLIA. He wouldn't come back. I followed him into

the big street and I called after him.   He didn't even turn his head.   Paddo is gone.

> *Nobody answers her.   There is silence which is only relieved by the sudden conflagration in the street outside as the bonfire blazes up and lights the inside of the place with flickering red lights.   They are all thinking their own thoughts,* WILLIE *very conscious of* LILY's *fingers against his cheek as the song of the kids dancing around the bonfire reaches into the room.   The kids are singing :*

'Up, darlin' Dovetail, he's the champeen of the right :
We'll folly him to battle 'neath the orange, green and white.
Next we'll tackle England and we'll show them how to fight,
And we'll crown darlin' Dovetail King of Ireland.'

### THE END

PRINTED BY R. & R. CLARK, LTD., EDINBURGH